WJEC Level 1/2 Vocational Award

Hospitality & Catering

There's a lot to cover in the WJEC Level 1/2 Vocational Award in Hospitality & Catering — and the revision experts are here to help with all of it!

This brilliant CGP Revision Guide explains all the important information you need for each unit of the course as clearly and concisely as possible.

There are also plenty of top tips and advice for the written exam and controlled assessment, all in CGP's classic style. It's a winner!

Unlock your Online Edition

Just scan the QR code below or go to **cgpbooks.co.uk/extras** and enter this code!

4302 0356 8843 1171

By the way, this code only works for one person. If somebody else has used this book before you, they might have already claimed the code.

Revision Guide

Contents

Getting Started
Course Overview 2

Unit 1: The Hospitality and Catering Industry

Section 1 — Hospitality and Catering Provision
Non-Commercial Provision 3
Commercial Provision 5
Types of Food Service 7
Standards and Ratings 9
Employment Roles — Front of House 10
Employment Roles — Housekeeping 11
Employment Roles — Kitchen Brigade 12
Employment Roles — Management 13
Qualifications and Experience 14
Contracts and Working Hours 15
Pay and Benefits 16
Costs and Profit 17
Economic Impacts 18
Environmental Impacts 19
The Impact of Technology 21
The Impact of Media 22
Revision Summary for Unit 1: Section 1 23

Section 2 — How Providers Operate
Operational Requirements 24
Equipment and Materials 27
Equipment, Materials and Dress Code 29
Administration and Documents 30
Meeting Customer Needs 33
Customer Expectations 36
Customer Demographics 37
Revision Summary for Unit 1: Section 2 38

Section 3 — Health & Safety
Health and Safety Laws 39
Accident Forms 41
Risk Assessments 42
Hazard Analysis and Critical Control Points 43

Section 4 — Food Safety
Food Hazards and Symptoms 45
Food Intolerances 46
Food Allergies and Food Poisoning 47
Preventing Food-Induced Ill-Health 48
Catering and the Law 51
Role of the EHO 52
Revision Summary for Unit 1: Sections 3 & 4 53

Unit 2: Hospitality and Catering in Action

Section 1 — The Importance of Nutrition
Nutrients and Fats 54
Proteins and Carbohydrates 55
Fibre, Water and Minerals 56
Vitamins 57
A Balanced Diet 58
Nutrition at Different Life-Stages 59
Special Dietary Needs — Lifestyle 61
Special Dietary Needs — Medical Conditions ... 62
Special Dietary Needs — Personal Beliefs 63
Revision Summary for Unit 2: Section 1 64

Section 2 — Menu Planning

Menu Planning and Costs 65
Customer Needs and Business Identity 66
Organoleptic Qualities 67
Dietary Requirements and Sustainability 68
Practical Requirements for Menu Planning 69
Planning Production 70
Revision Summary for Unit 2: Section 2 73

Section 3 — Skills and Techniques

Preparation and Knife Techniques 74
Cooking Techniques 76
Presentation Skills and Techniques 78
Food Safety Practices 80

Section 4 — Evaluating Cooking Skills

Reviewing Dishes 81
Reviewing Your Performance 82
Revision Summary for Unit 2: Sections 3 & 4 83

About the Assessments 84
Index 85

Published by CGP

Editors: Emily Forsberg, George Wright and Maddie Wright

Reviewer: Joanna Phillips

With thanks to Susan Alexander, Jennifer Bruce and Glenn Rogers for the proofreading.

With thanks to Jade Sim for the copyright research.

ISBN: 978 1 83774 144 1

Printed by Elanders Ltd, Newcastle upon Tyne.
Graphics from Corel® and Getty PA

Text, design, layout and original illustrations © Coordination Group Publications Ltd (CGP) 2024
All rights reserved.

Based on the classic CGP style created by Richard Parsons.

Photocopying more than one section of this book is not permitted, even if you have a CLA licence.
Extra copies are available from CGP with next day delivery • 0800 1712 712 • www.cgpbooks.co.uk

Course Overview

Read this page to get clued up on everything you'll come across during the Hospitality and Catering course.

The Course is Split into Two Units

As you can see in the Contents, this book is divided up into the sections that are listed here for each unit.

Unit 1: The Hospitality and Catering Industry

Unit 1 is divided into four sections:

1) HOSPITALITY AND CATERING PROVISION — you'll learn about the different types of establishments, what it's like to work in the hospitality and catering industry, and what makes a hospitality and catering provider successful.

2) HOW HOSPITALITY AND CATERING PROVISIONS OPERATE — this section covers how different teams within an establishment work to meet the needs and expectations of their customers.

3) HEALTH AND SAFETY IN HOSPITALITY AND CATERING — this section is about the different laws and practices that hospitality and catering establishments have to follow to keep their employees and customers safe.

4) FOOD SAFETY IN HOSPITALITY AND CATERING — the last section in Unit 1 covers the causes and symptoms of food-induced ill-health, and how an establishment can use control measures to prevent this.

For Unit 1, you'll sit an exam worth 80 marks. It lasts 1 hour and 20 minutes, and is worth 40% of the qualification.

Unit 2: Hospitality and Catering in Action

Unit 2 is also divided into four sections:

1) THE IMPORTANCE OF NUTRITION — you'll learn about the function of different nutrients and how different groups of people have different nutritional needs. You'll also cover how cooking methods can affect the nutritional value of food.

2) MENU PLANNING — this section is all about the factors you need to consider when planning a menu, and how to create a useful production plan to help your time in the kitchen run smoothly and safely.

3) SKILLS AND TECHNIQUES — this section covers lots of skills and techniques you might need when preparing, cooking and presenting dishes.

4) EVALUATING COOKING SKILLS — this final section gives some areas you can discuss when asked to review your cooking and performance in the controlled assessment.

Unit 2 is examined through a controlled assessment that is split into four tasks, worth a total of 120 marks. You'll also need to draw upon Unit 1 knowledge in the controlled assessment. You'll be given 12 hours in total to complete all the tasks. The controlled assessment is worth 60% of the qualification.

There's more detail of what the exam and controlled assessment will involve on page 84.

Course Overview — starter, main, side dish and dessert...

My stomach is rumbling from writing this page. Before you start, I should warn you that taking this course may make you very hungry. It'll be worth it though — you'll be a hospitality and catering expert by the end...

Unit 1: Section 1 — Hospitality and Catering Provision

Non-Commercial Provision

Establishments in the hospitality and catering industry aim to provide a friendly service to customers, guests and visitors. You need to know about the different types of hospitality and catering service providers.

Hospitality and Catering is all about Providing a Service

1) Hospitality and catering services offer things like accommodation, food and drink, and entertainment.
2) Hospitality establishments provide more than one of these services, such as a holiday resort.
3) Catering establishments serve food and drink.
   Examples include cafés, school canteens, hotel restaurants and wine bars.

Establishments can be Commercial or Non-Commercial...

Commercial

1) Commercial establishments (see pages 5-6) sell their services and aim to make a profit.
2) Examples include a restaurant or a bed and breakfast.

Non-Commercial

1) Non-commercial establishments do not aim to make a profit from their services.
2) Examples include a prison canteen or a hospital cafeteria.

...and Residential or Non-Residential

- Residential establishments provide accommodation for their customers and often provide food and drink. For example, a bed and breakfast or a hotel.
- Non-residential catering establishments don't provide accommodation for customers. For example, a restaurant, a café or a staff canteen.

Non-Commercial Establishments can be Residential

1) These are establishments that:
   - Offer accommodation.
   - Do not aim to make a profit.

2) Instead of making a profit, the main aim of these establishments depends on what the needs of their visitors and residents are.

3) E.g. the main aims of a boarding school are to educate and look after students. To look after their students, they must provide catering and accommodation.

Joke writer at your service — I cater for all your comedy needs...

Make sure you know the difference between commercial and non-commercial establishments.
Ooh and don't forget about residential and non-residential establishments too.

Non-Commercial Provision

You need to know some Examples of Residential Provisions

There are four types of non-commercial residential establishments that you need to know about:

1) Hospitals, hospices and care homes
   - The main aim of these establishments is to provide care to people who are ill or can't live independently.
   - Accommodation and food are provided as part of this service.

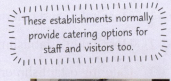
These establishments normally provide catering options for staff and visitors too.

2) Boarding schools, colleges and university residences
   - Accommodation is provided for students who live on-site.
   - Most places provide a full catering service for students who want it.
   - Universities may offer the choice of self-catering accommodation, which comes with a kitchen for students to cook their own meals.
   - Housekeeping may be provided, or students may have to clean their own living areas.

3) Armed forces
   - In the UK, chefs in the British Army, the Royal Air Force and the Royal Navy are normally responsible for sourcing ingredients and preparing meals.
   - Accommodation is available close to places of work for people in the armed forces and their families. They may have to move location regularly.

4) Prisons
   - Prison caterers make and serve food and drink to inmates.

Non-Commercial Establishments can also be Non-Residential

1) These are establishments that:
   - Do not offer accommodation.
   - Do not aim to make a profit.

2) You need to know some examples of non-residential establishments:

   1) Canteens in places of work
      - In places like hospitals, supermarkets, and offices, food can be provided for workers.
      - The food is often subsidised — the employer pays towards the cost of the food to make it cheaper for workers.

   2) Schools, colleges and universities
      - Canteens in places of education provide subsidised food and drink for students.
      - They might prepare the meals on-site, or the meals may get delivered by a catering company.

   3) Meals on wheels
      - These are services for people who live at home but have difficulty cooking for themselves.
      - Hot meals are prepared and delivered directly to eligible people's homes.

   4) Charity-run food providers
      - Food is donated to food banks, and organisations give it out to those in need.
      - Soup kitchens prepare free meals for those who can't afford to feed themselves.

I eat my breakfast whilst skateboarding — it's meals on wheels...

You might notice that some places like universities offer both residential and non-residential options. This is good because it means they can cater for lots of guests with different needs.

Unit 1: Section 1 — Hospitality and Catering Provision

Commercial Provision

These next two pages are all about hospitality and catering services that aim to make a profit.

Commercial Residential Establishments are Places like Hotels

Commercial residential establishments are businesses that:
- Offer accommodation.
- Aim to make a profit.

Hotels
1) Rooms can be different sizes, e.g. single, double, king or family-sized, and have an en-suite bathroom.
2) They can offer a range of dining options, such as table-service (see p.7) meals or room service.
3) Hotels in lots of countries are given a star rating out of five stars, to show the quality of their service.
4) They may offer leisure facilities, such as a gym, spa or swimming pool.
5) Some hotels have larger rooms for functions like weddings or conferences. They may cater for weddings and provide the equipment needed for conferences, like a projector, pens, paper and refreshments.

Motels
1) Motels offer basic accommodation similar to hotel rooms. They are usually located close to a main road and most of their customers are drivers on long journeys.
2) They might have a restaurant offering breakfast and dinner options.

Hostels
1) Most rooms in hostels are shared, and each guest pays for their own bed within the room.
2) Hostels normally have shared bathrooms and communal living spaces.
3) They normally have a kitchen that guests can use to prepare their own food.

Holiday Parks
1) Holiday parks offer a range of leisure activities, dining options and accommodation on one site.
2) Dining options may include restaurants, cafés, pubs and takeaways.
3) Accommodation options might include lodges, cabins or pods.

B&Bs, Guest Houses and Airbnbs
1) B&Bs (bed and breakfasts) and guest houses are smaller than hotels and offer accommodation and breakfast. They might also have communal areas. Bathrooms may be shared or en-suite.
2) Airbnb is an online platform where a home owner can rent out a bedroom or a whole property.

Campsites and Caravan Parks
1) These are spaces for campers to set up tents, camper vans and caravans which they bring themselves.
2) Facilities provided usually include showers, toilets and electricity stations.

Cruise Ships
1) Cruise ships have hotel-like rooms and cater for guests throughout their time on-board.
2) They usually have lots of dining options such as banquet-style restaurants and buffets (see p.7-8).
3) They have a range of leisure activities on-board and may organise tours and day-trips off the ship.

Oooh and there's also cosmotels — hotels in space...
...for some reason they don't ever seem to come up in the exam, though. Make sure you know the seven types of establishments on this page, and the facilities and catering options that each of them provides.

Unit 1: Section 1 — Hospitality and Catering Provision

Commercial Provision

Commercial Non-Residential Provisions aren't just Restaurants

1) Non-residential establishments in the commercial sector are ones that:
   - Don't offer accommodation.
   - Aim to make a profit.

2) Some commercial non-residential businesses focus only on serving food and drink, e.g. restaurants.

3) Others might provide a different service, such as entertainment or transport. They serve food and drink as an extra service. E.g. football stadiums host matches for entertainment but also have food stands.

Establishments sell Different Types of Food

1) The type of food on offer and the way it is served depends on what the customer wants.

2) Lots of different non-residential places offer catering services to make a profit:

Tearooms, Cafés and Coffee Shops
- These are often casual settings that serve a range of beverages, light meals and snacks.
- Customers might order at the counter, or some places offer full table service.

Airlines and Long-Distance Trains
- Food and drinks are usually available for customers to purchase on-board. These are usually provided by trolley service (see p.8). For long-haul journeys, a meal service is often included in the price of a ticket.
- On a plane, customers are served at their seat. Trains might have an extra dining carriage.

Fast Food and Takeaways
- These are places that offer made-to-order food that is usually eaten elsewhere.
- Fast food is ordered at a counter and prepared quickly. It is usually a much cheaper option than eating at a restaurant.
- Customers normally order takeaways online or over the phone. There's more on how takeaway service works on page 8.

Restaurants and Bistros
- Waiting staff serve food to the table.
- Bistros are often smaller than restaurants and tend to be more casual and sometimes cheaper.
- Pop-up restaurants operate in different locations for short periods of time. They usually offer unique dining experiences.

Stadia, Concert Halls and Tourist Attractions
- A range of food and drink is provided at different locations, such as food stalls, mobile food trucks and table-service spots.

Vending Machines
- These are cabinets that display packaged snacks and drinks for customers to buy.
- They offer cheap, convenient, quick options for customers.
- They can be found in places like train stations, airports and hospitals.

Pubs and Bars
- Pubs and bars have a licence to serve alcohol to customers over the age of 18.
- They might also offer table-service meals.

I don't really like plane food — it never tastes of anything...

Make sure you know the seven types of commercial non-residential establishments on this page. You could have a go at comparing them. E.g. restaurants need waiting staff and tend to be more expensive than fast food.

Unit 1: Section 1 — Hospitality and Catering Provision

Types of Food Service

Food can be served in lots of different ways and it often depends on the type of establishment. Food service has been mentioned a few times already on the previous pages, but there's a lot more detail about it here...

Table Service is Common in Restaurants

1) Table service is when waiters and waitresses take customers' orders and deliver their food to the table.
2) It's used in places such as restaurants, cafés and hotels, or at large functions such as wedding receptions.
3) Here are five different types of table service:

PLATE SERVICE

- Plate service is where food is plated in the kitchen by the chef and taken to the table by waiting staff.
- This means the portion sizes of each dish will be similar, and ensures guests are served quickly, whilst the food is still hot.

In fine dining restaurants, the presentation of each dish is completed by a skilled chef. It is seen as a work of art.

GUÉRIDON SERVICE

- In guéridon service a chef or trained server finishes the preparation or cooking at the customer's table.
- This entertains customers because they can watch the member of staff show off their skills.
- The member of staff needs to be able to 'perform', and it usually requires specialist equipment.

SILVER SERVICE

- Waiting staff serve food from a large dish onto the customer's plate, at their table.
- Waiting staff use a spoon and fork in a specific way to serve the food, which requires skill and training. Traditionally, the dish, fork and spoon used by waiting staff were all silver — this is where the name 'silver service' comes from.
- It's a luxury dining service that's normally used in high-end restaurants and hotels.

BANQUET

- A banquet is a formal meal that usually has a lot of guests and can involve lots of courses.
- Banquets are often held at celebratory events such as weddings and ceremonies.
- Guests might choose their food before the event, usually from a small number of options.
- They can be served using different service styles, such as plate, silver or buffet (see next page).
- Banquets normally require a lot of waiting staff.

FAMILY-STYLE

- A family-style meal is where waiting staff bring lots of large serving dishes to the table for everyone on the table to share.
- The customers serve themselves from the large dishes, so they can choose their own portion sizes.

Tennis players make great waiting staff — they are excellent servers...

Who knew there were so many ways that you could get your food served at a table?
And that's not all — there are lots more ways that food can be served on the next page...

Unit 1: Section 1 — Hospitality and Catering Provision

Types of Food Service

Customers Take Their Food to the Table in Counter Service

Counter service is usually a quick and convenient option for customers.
It is also good for the establishment as they can serve a lot of customers in a short time.

Cafeteria Service

- Food and drink are placed on long food counters. Customers walk along the counters and pick up the food they want. They pay at a till, collect cutlery and take it to their table.
- It is commonly used in school and workplace canteens, and in some cafés.

Buffet Service

- Customers can choose from lots of serving dishes containing a variety of food.
- Customers can plate up their own food or there might be staff behind the counter to do it for them. They can go back to the food counter as many times as they wish.
- Buffets are common at hotel breakfast services.
- Customers pay a set amount per person for the meal.

Kelly thought it was a table service restaurant...

Fast Food Service

- At a fast-food outlet, food is cooking all the time using specialist kitchen equipment. This allows the food to be served quickly, and it is often served in disposable packaging.
- The menu can be quite limited and is normally displayed on a board behind the counter.
- Customers can find their own table or take their food elsewhere.

Personal Service is where Food is Given Directly to the Customer

Tray or Trolley

1) Customers are served food on a tray or trolley. They sometimes order the food in advance.
2) This is often used on aeroplanes, long-haul trains and for hotel room service.

Home Delivery and Takeaway

1) Customers order their food over the phone, online or on an app.
2) For a takeaway, the customer collects their food when it is ready.
3) For home delivery, the establishment organises for orders to be delivered to customers' homes.

Vending Service

1) Customers purchase food directly from vending machines (see page 6).
2) People are needed to restock the vending machines, and keep them clean and serviced.

I couldn't keep up with my burger and fries — they were too fast...

Establishments have to choose the right style of service for the type of customers they get. For example, a customer in a fast-food shop is probably looking for a quick meal, so wouldn't want to wait for table service.

Standards and Ratings

The ratings given to hospitality and catering establishments tell customers what they can expect from the service there. Places that serve food are also rated for their hygiene standards.

Hotels and Guest Houses are Rated out of Five Stars

1) Achieving a good rating is important for all commercial hospitality and catering businesses, as it can attract new customers. Customers are also happy to pay more for a higher quality service.
2) The AA is a British motoring association that gives hotels and guest houses in the UK a star rating.
3) Their award is nationally credited, and it is based on the service and facilities offered by the establishment.
4) Establishments are given a rating out of five, with five stars being awarded to the best accommodation. The table below shows some features that hotels and guest houses must offer for each award:

Star Rating	Criteria
★	Staff offer an informal service, rooms are basic, breakfast is served daily. The minimum requirements are met for cleanliness and facilities. Hotel rooms must be en-suite.
★★	Staff offer a courteous service and beds are well-maintained. Hotels must have a dining area serving breakfast and dinner most days. Guest houses must offer breakfast.
★★★	Staff are friendly and helpful. Rooms are well-presented. Hotels must have a restaurant serving a range of breakfast and dinner options. Hotel rooms should have free Wi-Fi.
★★★★	Staff offer a professional, personalised service. Hotels must have 24/7 room service and offer enhanced services like afternoon tea. Half of guest house rooms must be en-suite.
★★★★★	Luxury accommodation with high-quality food options. Hotel staff speak multiple languages and there are extra services like valet parking. All guest house rooms are en-suite.

There are Different Awards for Food Services

Michelin Star

- Michelin is a company that gives awards to top restaurants in the world for the quality of the dishes they create.
- A Michelin star is a renowned award that many chefs dedicate their careers to achieve.
- A restaurant can be awarded up to three Michelin stars, for the highest quality food.

AA Rosette Awards

- The AA awards hotels and restaurants in the UK up to five rosettes for the quality of food they offer.
- Restaurants often apply to be considered for a rosette award, as it can help attract customers.

Good Food Guide

- The Good Food Guide is a company that rates the best places to eat out in Britain. It gives establishments a rating from 'Good', 'Very Good', 'Exceptional' or 'World Class'.
- It also gives out awards, in categories like 'Best Local Restaurant' and 'Best New Restaurant'.

Food Hygiene Ratings

- The Food Standards Agency gives every place serving food in the UK a hygiene rating from 0-5. A rating of 5 means they have the best hygiene standards that comply with the law.
- A low rating means they have poor hygiene which needs improving for safety reasons. Poor ratings can put off customers from visiting.

I got a five-star rating from the AA — I'm a really good driver...

Ratings are really important in the hospitality and catering industry. Low standards and ratings can put a lot of customers off using a service. For commercial establishments, this means they might not make a profit.

Employment Roles — Front of House

There are four main areas in the hospitality and catering industry, which are covered on the next four pages.

Front of House Staff have Direct Contact with Customers

1) Front of house employees are those that have customer-facing roles, such as receptionists and waiting staff. Because of this, they should be friendly and smart, to help to promote a positive image.
2) They also need to have strong customer service and communication skills. Customers go to front of house staff if they have a problem, so they need to be proactive in helping to sort any issues.
3) The front of house is often set up as a hierarchical structure — the front of house manager is at the top of the structure and has the most authority. Other roles below them have different levels of authority.
4) You need to know the following front of house roles, and the attributes that employers look for:

Front of House Manager

Hires and trains front of house staff. Ensures staff do their jobs to a high standard.
- Organised — they may have a large number of staff to oversee.
- Approachable — staff should be comfortable going to them with any problems they have.

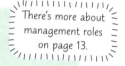
There's more about management roles on page 13.

Head Waiter and Maître d'Hôtel

Responsible for greeting customers, organising and training waiting staff, and handling complaints.
- Leadership qualities — need to be able to look after lots of waiting staff.
- Calm and resourceful — they may need to solve problems quickly to keep customers happy.

Waiting Staff

Seats guests, takes their orders, serves food and takes payments. Cleans dining areas.
- Willing to learn — they need to have a good knowledge of the menu to pass on to guests.
- Calm and a team player — it is a fast-paced job and they should be happy to help colleagues.

Concierge

Helps guests book tourist attractions, dinner reservations and taxis in the local area.
- Willing to learn — needs to be knowledgeable about the local area.

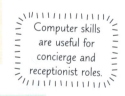
Computer skills are useful for concierge and receptionist roles.

Receptionist

Takes bookings, checks guests in and deals with any customer questions and complaints.
- Flexible and organised — they need to be able to do lots of different jobs.
- Good listener — guests may have a variety of things they need help with.

Valet

Welcomes guests to the establishment and parks their cars.
- Friendly and well-presented — often the first members of staff that guests will meet.

Front of house — also known as the porch...

There's lots to learn on this page — start by seeing if you can remember what all of the roles are.
Then have a think about the different qualities in a person that would make them good at each role.

Employment Roles — Housekeeping

Places with Accommodation have a Housekeeping Team

1) The main purpose of the housekeeping team is to make sure an establishment is kept clean and tidy, and ensure that everything works properly.

2) There are lots of attributes that employers might look for when recruiting housekeeping staff:

- Punctual — bedrooms in hotels need to be ready for new guests before check-in time, so it is important staff arrive to work on time.
- Flexible and organised — some jobs might be more urgent than others, so they should be able to prioritise their tasks. E.g. fixing a broken shower is more important than replacing a broken light bulb in a lamp.
- Hard-working and a team player — there is often a lot to do, and staff should be willing to help their colleagues.
- Well-presented and friendly — although not a front of house role, housekeeping staff work in public areas so it is important they look presentable and are polite to guests.

There are Different Housekeeping Roles

CHAMBERMAID

1) Chambermaids prepare bedrooms for new guests.

2) They change the bedding and towels, clean the room and replace any used products like shampoo and tea bags.

3) Some places offer this service every day during a guest's stay, whilst others may only do it at the start of each check-in.

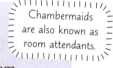
Chambermaids are also known as room attendants.

CLEANER

1) Cleans public areas of an establishment, such as leisure facilities, hallways and public toilets.

2) Includes vacuuming, mopping and dusting.

MAINTENANCE

1) Repairs any machines or equipment in the establishment that break.

2) Maintains the interior and exterior of the building, e.g. by painting walls and cleaning windows.

3) If something is broken that requires a specialist to fix, such as a boiler, they might have to arrange for an expert to have a look at it.

CARETAKER

1) Similar to maintenance staff, caretakers make sure the building and its grounds are in good condition.

2) Caretakers are usually responsible for the security of the building — they might hold keys for different parts of the building and lock it at night.

Did you hear about the cleaner who got famous...

... they're sweeping the nation. Not every business will have exactly the same housekeeping roles. Large, busy hotels often have employees who just have one job to take care of, such as gardening or laundry.

Unit 1: Section 1 — Hospitality and Catering Provision

Employment Roles — Kitchen Brigade

The Kitchen Brigade is the Back of House

- The kitchen brigade is a framework used for hiring kitchen staff. It is most commonly found in professional kitchens in restaurants and hotels, where there are multiple elements that are needed to create a meal.
- The framework helps the kitchen run efficiently. Each role comes with very specific jobs, and every job is an important step to creating dishes for customers. This means everyone in a kitchen must have excellent teamwork and communication skills.

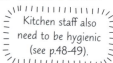
Kitchen staff also need to be hygienic (see p.48-49).

- Kitchens are fast-paced, so employees need to be calm, organised and able to work under pressure.

The Structure is a Hierarchy

1) Like in the front of house team, each role in the kitchen brigade has a different level of authority.
2) The roles in a kitchen brigade are described below, in order from most senior to least senior:

Executive / Head Chef
Plans the menu and ensures the kitchen has all the ingredients and equipment they need. Hires and trains staff, and ensures dishes are made to a high standard. They are responsible for health and safety in the kitchen. This is the most senior role in the hierarchy, so comes with the most authority (see p.13 for more on management attributes). It requires the most skill and training to be an executive chef.

Sous-Chef
The sous-chef is the second in command in the kitchen and is responsible for overseeing kitchen staff. They are in charge when the executive chef is busy with their other responsibilities.

Chef de Party

Chef de Partie
In charge of one area of the kitchen, e.g. sauce, soup, vegetables, fish. The sauce chef is the most senior of all the chefs de partie.

Pastry Chef
The pastry chef makes pastries, desserts and bread. Sometimes the pastry chef is responsible for the dessert menu.

Commis Chef
Commis chefs are training to become a chef, and help other chefs with the easiest tasks. They work in all the different areas of the kitchen to improve their skills.

Kitchen Assistant
Helps with simple jobs like washing, chopping, peeling and cutting ingredients. They might also help with keeping work stations tidy.

Apprentice
Might be training in multiple areas or just one area of the kitchen during an apprenticeship (see p.14).

Kitchen Porter or Plongeur
Washes dishes and cooking equipment. Cleans down the kitchen at the end of service.

The kitchen brigade were ready for battle — the 6pm dinner service...

Most people who want to be a chef start out near the bottom of the hierarchy. Once they have practised and mastered the skills, they might slowly work their way up and could one day become an executive chef.

Unit 1: Section 1 — Hospitality and Catering Provision

Employment Roles — Management

Management Oversee other Employees

1) Each department within a hospitality and catering establishment needs at least one manager — these are people who delegate jobs to staff within their team and make sure that everyone has what they need to do their jobs to a high standard.

2) Managers ensure everything in the establishment runs smoothly.

3) There are lots of attributes that make a good manager, for example:

- Good communicator
- Organised
- Approachable
- Attention to detail
- Hardworking
- Leadership qualities

Food and Beverage Manager Oversees the Front of House and Kitchen

1) Oversees the work of everyone in the food and beverage team and makes sure jobs are completed to sufficient standards.

2) Manages the establishment's bookings — too many bookings could mean staff are overworked. But not enough bookings will mean the establishment makes less money.

3) Pays any bills the establishment owes, like water and rent.
Makes sure the establishment isn't spending too much.

4) Orders stock such as napkins and glasses, and makes sure the store cupboard is well-stocked.

5) Makes sure customers are happy with their experience at the establishment.

The Housekeeping Team also has a Manager

- Keeps on top of the laundering of bedding and towels, and checks the rooms.
- Orders stock such as soap, tea and coffee for guests to use in the room.
Also orders cleaning products and equipment for chambermaids and cleaners to use.
- Ensures the housekeeping team follow health and safety procedures.
- Allocates room numbers to room attendants and checks everything is cleaned properly.
- Tells reception when rooms are ready for new guests.

The Marketing Manager Takes Care of Advertising

1) Aims to attract new customers and get previous customers to return.
2) Responsible for advertising the establishment, e.g. through social media and emails.
3) Keeps their website up to date.
4) Promotes special offers and discounts.

Managers do lots of overseeing — travelling across the Caribbean...

Managers have a lot of responsibility — they are responsible for the success of their team. If their team does a bad job, it can have a big impact on the success of the whole establishment. No pressure then...

Unit 1: Section 1 — Hospitality and Catering Provision

Qualifications and Experience

Gaining work experience or qualifications is a great way to show employers you have the skills needed to work in the hospitality and catering sector. They can also help you get a higher-paid role with more responsibilities.

Work Experience Helps you Gain Skills

1) You can learn the skills needed for working in the sector by doing some work experience.

2) This can be a part-time or temporary job, e.g. during school holidays, when establishments are busy and need extra help.

3) Often, no previous experience is required. Learning often happens on-the-job.

4) Work experience is a good way to see if you like working in the sector, before committing to a full-time job or career in hospitality and catering.

5) You can also gain experience by doing an apprenticeship:

Apprenticeships

An apprenticeship is a paid job combined with classroom learning.

- Lots of restaurants and hotels offer apprenticeships for a range of roles.
- Working in the sector helps you gain skills and experience.
- Apprenticeships are available at different levels, and take 1 to 5 years to complete.
- You gain a nationally recognised qualification.

Some Roles Require you to have Qualifications

1) Qualifications can be gained by studying on a school, college or university course.

2) They involve classroom study and assessment. Examples include:

Schools and Colleges

- GCSE English, Maths, Business, Food Preparation and Nutrition, Hospitality and Catering, etc.
- Level 1/2 Vocational Award in Hospitality and Catering.
- Level 1/2 Certificate in Business and Administration, Front of House Reception, etc.
- BTEC in Hospitality, Catering, Business, etc.

Universities

- Bachelor's degree in Hospitality and Hotel Management, Catering, etc.
- Higher National Certificate (HNC) or Higher National Diploma (HND) in Professional Cookery, Hospitality Management, Culinary Arts, Food and Beverage Service, etc.

Apprenticeships aren't easy — I'd start with a smaller boat first...

Work experience and apprenticeships are a great way to show employers you have real-world experience working in the hospitality and catering industry — previous experience may be required for some roles.

Unit 1: Section 1 — Hospitality and Catering Provision

Contracts and Working Hours

A contract explains the responsibilities, hours, pay and benefits of a role — you need to know the different types.

A Contract Sets Out Job Requirements

A contract is an agreement between the employer and employee that sets out what a job involves. There are different types of contract, and they each have advantages and disadvantages:

Full-time

Employees have a fixed number of hours each week and work all year round. The contract is often permanent. A full-time temporary contract means they work every week for a fixed period, e.g. 6 months.

Advantages:
- Entitled to holidays and sick pay.
- Receive a salary and a pension (see p.16).

Disadvantages:
- Hard to balance for people who have other commitments, e.g. a single parent or a student.

Part-time

Similar to a full-time contract, but employees only work on certain days of the week, or for fewer hours. They are paid pro-rata (proportional to the number of hours they work).

Advantages:
- Good for people who have other commitments.
- Still receive benefits, e.g. sick pay and a pension.

Disadvantages:
- May receive fewer benefits.
- Paid less than a full-time position.

Seasonal

A temporary role offered when an establishment needs more staff, e.g. during school holidays.

Advantages:
- Good for students who are busy during term times.
- Flexible hours may be available.

Disadvantages:
- May not receive benefits.
- The employer doesn't have to offer them a job for the next season.

Part-time and seasonal positions are common in the hospitality and catering industry because some times of the day or year are busier than others, e.g. Christmas.

Zero-hours and Casual Contracts

Zero-hours contracts are where the employee only works when the employer needs them. Casual contracts are usually offered to cover other employees who are on sick leave, or during busy periods.

Advantages:
- It is flexible — employees can work when they are free and employers don't have to offer work if it isn't needed.

Disadvantages:
- Usually don't get sick pay or holiday entitlement.
- Employer may be stuck if the job isn't accepted, or employee may need work but isn't offered any.

The Working Times Regulations (1998) in the UK state that:
1) A worker cannot work for more than an average of 48 hours a week, unless they choose to.
2) People under 18 can't work for more than 8 hours a day or 40 hours a week.
3) If shifts are over 6 hours, an employee must be given a 20-minute break and at least 1 day off a week.

Zero-hours contracts are good for gymnasts — they're very flexible...

An employer might have workers on a range of contracts to make sure they can cater for the fluctuating needs of the industry. E.g. a restaurant needs more waiting staff at work during dinner time than in the afternoon.

Pay and Benefits

Remuneration just means the money that is paid to an employee for the work that they do. Depending on their contract, employees can also receive a range of benefits and rewards.

Employees can get a Salary or a Wage

1) A salary is a fixed amount paid every month — this doesn't change even if the number of hours worked changes. It is usually paid to employees on full-time or part-time contracts. A salary of £24 000 means you are paid £2000 each month.

2) A wage is where employees are paid for the number of hours they work — this is often used for employees on contracts where the number of hours worked varies greatly from week to week, e.g. a zero-hours contract. Someone who works 6 hours at a rate of £12 per hour is paid £72.

Employers must Pay at least the Minimum Wage

- To protect workers from being underpaid, the UK government sets National Minimum Wage rates — this is the legal minimum amount that employers must pay their employees per hour.
- The rates are reviewed and changed yearly to reflect changes in the cost of living.
- It varies depending on the age of the employee. E.g. in April 2024, National Minimum Wage rates were:

Employee age	Minimum hourly wage (£)
21 and over	11.44
18 to 20	8.60
under 18	6.40
apprentice rate	6.40

The rate for workers aged 21 or over is called the National Living Wage.

The apprentice rate is for apprentices under 19, and those over 19 in the first year of their apprenticeship.

Employees may Receive Extra Benefits

Holiday Entitlement

Full-time workers are entitled to 28 days of paid holiday per year. Part-time workers also have some holiday entitlement, worked out on a pro-rata basis.

Sick Pay

Some types of contract also mean the employee still gets paid even if they can't go in to work due to illness.

Pensions

A pension agreement means the employer and government contribute towards funds for the employee. The employee has access to these funds when they reach retirement age.

Bonuses and Rewards

An employer might give employees extra money on top of their regular payments to show appreciation for the workers' efforts. They might also give other benefits, such as vouchers for food or accommodation. This might happen at the end of a year, or after a busy period for the establishment.

Tips

Customers often give extra money to employees for their good service. This is common for waiting staff in restaurants and front of house staff in hotels.

I used to work at a salad bar but the monthly celery wasn't enough...

Benefits don't just have to be money — for example, some establishments might provide free or subsidised food for their employees. Others might provide healthcare benefits or pay towards their transport to work.

Costs and Profit

There are three basic costs for hospitality and catering provisions that you need to know about.
A commercial establishment can use their costs to calculate whether or not they are making a profit.

There are Three Basic Costs for Businesses

A commercial establishment needs to decide how much they should charge for their service.
They need to consider everything they spend money on to make sure they make a profit:

Labour

The total amount paid by a business in wages, payroll taxes and the cost of any employee benefits.

- Labour costs vary depending on the level of authority and the skills needed for each role. For example, an executive chef will have a higher wage than an assistant chef.
- Labour costs may also change when there are changes to the National Minimum Wage (see p.16).
- The owner of the business also has to make a living, so their wage is included in labour costs.

Materials

The materials needed for hospitality and catering are mostly consumables — this just means anything that gets used up by customers or employees that needs replacing regularly.

- Catering establishments need to buy ingredients and drinks, as well as things like menus, napkins and cleaning materials.
- Materials needed by residential establishments include things like soap, shampoo and any other products they offer in their rooms. They also need cleaning materials.

Overheads

Regular bills the business has to pay to continue running, such as rent, electricity, water and gas. It also includes additional costs for things like furniture and the maintenance of equipment.

- An establishment should make sure they are able to pay their bills on time.
- They should be prepared to pay for any unexpected repairs, such as for a broken oven.

Profit is Sales Minus Costs

Gross Profit:
- Gross Profit = Sales − Food Costs
- The difference between the amount it costs to make a dish and the amount it sells for.
  - E.g. if a dish costs £4 to make and sells for £12, it has a gross profit of £8.
  - It is normally calculated as a total of all food and drink items sold in, e.g. a year.

Net Profit:
- Net Profit = Sales − All Costs
- Takes into account costs of labour, materials and overheads.
- The amount left over from gross profit after all costs have been considered.

My three basic costs — tea, biscuits and a good joke...

If a business has costs that are higher than their sales, then profit is negative — this means they are making a loss. They might look at ways to increases sales or decrease costs in order to make a profit.

Unit 1: Section 1 — Hospitality and Catering Provision

Economic Impacts

The hospitality and catering industry is very competitive. The next five pages look at the factors affecting a business in this industry. To make a profit and be successful, a business must adapt to these changing factors.

People Spend More when the Economy is Strong

- Disposable income is the amount of money someone has left after they have paid for food, bills, taxes and other basic needs. They can choose what to do with this money.
- The strength of the economy affects how much disposable income people have:

Strong Economy
1) People have more disposable income.
2) They spend more on leisure activities and eating out.
3) This is good for businesses in the hospitality and catering industry — they are more likely to make a profit.

Weak Economy
1) People have less disposable income.
2) They spend less on leisure and eating out.
3) This makes it harder for hospitality and catering businesses to make a profit.

In a weak economy, the cost of things like electricity, gas and food may increase, which can increase costs to businesses and affect profits.

Value Added Tax (VAT) is Added to Most Sales

1) In the UK, VAT is added to the cost of any product or service that is considered non-essential or a luxury. This includes most things in the hospitality and catering sector, such as a meal out or a hotel stay.
2) VAT is paid by customers and is currently 20% of the cost for most services and prepared food.
3) VAT goes directly to the government and is used to pay for public services like the NHS and education.

The Value of the Pound affects the Industry

- An exchange rate is the price at which one currency can be traded for another.
- When the exchange rate is good for the pound, other currencies are cheaper to buy and the pound is strong.
- When the exchange rate is poor for the pound, other currencies cost more to buy and the pound is weak.

Cost of Ingredients
1) A lot of ingredients used in the UK hospitality and catering industry are imported from other countries, e.g. because the UK does not have the right climate for them to grow.
2) When the pound is weak, it is more expensive to import things from abroad, so costs are higher and it is harder to make a profit.
3) When the pound is strong, it is cheaper to import things from abroad, so costs are lower and it is easier to make a profit.

Number of Customers
1) When the pound is weak, it benefits people from abroad — it is good value for them to holiday in the UK so they will spend more on hospitality and catering.
2) People from the UK are also less likely to holiday abroad, so may spend their holiday in the UK instead. This is good for the UK hospitality and catering industry, as people will spend their money at home rather than in another country.

I think I've really misunderstood what disposable income is...
... I put all of mine in the bin. At least I recycled it. Speaking of recycling, there's a bit about environmental impacts on businesses coming up next. But don't move on until you've mastered the economic impacts.

Unit 1: Section 1 — Hospitality and Catering Provision

Environmental Impacts

Many people like to look after the environment these days. The hospitality and catering industry is no different.

Carbon Footprint Measures Environmental Impact

- Greenhouse gases, such as carbon dioxide, are released into the atmosphere by lots of human processes. This contributes to climate change, which is bad for the environment.
- The carbon footprint of a process is the amount of greenhouse gases it releases into the atmosphere.
- The carbon footprint of a dish in a restaurant is made up of all the steps the ingredients go through to produce the dish:

  1) Growing or farming 3) Packaging 5) Cooking
  2) Processing 4) Transporting 6) Disposing of waste

- Reducing the carbon footprint of any of these six steps can help to make a business more sustainable — this means using Earth's resources more responsibly and having lower environmental impact.
- There are lots of ways a business can do this, covered in detail below and on the next page:

  1) Choosing foods with lower food miles — reduces carbon footprint of transporting.
  2) Saving energy and water — reduces carbon footprint of cooking.
  3) Reducing waste — reduces carbon footprint of packaging and disposing of waste.

Seasonal Ingredients have Low Food Miles

1) Seasonal ingredients, such as strawberries, can only be grown at certain times of year in the UK, and some foods can't be grown commercially in the UK, e.g. bananas.

2) Lots of customers expect these foods to be available all year round, so businesses may feel pressure to import them from other countries. Importing from other countries can sometimes be cheaper too.

3) However, this means some food is transported a long way, e.g. some green beans eaten in the UK have come from Kenya. These foods have high food miles:

Food Miles — the distance food travels from where it's produced to the consumer.

4) Using lots of foods with high food miles is bad for the environment — planes, ships and trucks all burn scarce fossil fuels and release carbon dioxide into the atmosphere.

5) Local, seasonal foods have much lower food miles than ingredients imported from abroad, so they are usually better for the environment. They are often fresher and tastier too.

6) Catering businesses might choose local and seasonal ingredients to become more sustainable. They might have to change their menu regularly, depending on which seasonal foods are available.

It's not just food miles that affect how environmentally friendly an ingredient is. For example, using more plant-based ingredients and fewer animal products can help reduce carbon footprint.

From plate to mouth — 0.0001 food miles...

The carbon footprint of a dish is really hard to measure because ~~bananas don't have feet~~ there are so many complex steps that need to be considered. But reducing food miles is a good way it can be reduced.

Environmental Impacts

There are ways to Save Energy and Water

1) Businesses can also be more sustainable by saving energy and water. There are lots of ways to do this:

In Kitchens
- Use the correct sized pan and hob.
- Put lids on pans.
- Don't boil more water than you need.
- Fully load dishwashers.
- Cook some foods together (this may depend on customer allergies, see p.47).

In Accommodation
- Use energy-efficient appliances.
- Fully load washing machines.
- Reduce the number of times bedding is changed for each visitor.
- Carry out maintenance checks to ensure everything is working efficiently.

Using renewable energy sources, such as solar power, instead of fossil fuels is another way businesses can become more sustainable.

2) Saving water reduces the energy needed for processing and delivering it to buildings for humans to use. Generating energy usually releases greenhouse gases, so saving energy can be a good way for a business to reduce its carbon footprint.

3) It can also save money and help businesses build a good reputation with their customers.

Businesses should try to Reduce Waste

- Reducing waste is another way that a hospitality and catering business can become more sustainable — e.g. less waste may be sent to landfill and fewer new resources may be needed to make new products.
- They can use the three Rs to reduce their waste:

1) Reduce — cut down on packaging waste and food waste by:
   - Ordering in bulk, e.g. one big bag of potatoes instead of lots of little bags.
   - Choose suppliers that use biodegradable packaging (rots naturally in the ground).
   - Rotate stock to avoid it going out of date, and only buy the amount of fresh food that's needed.
   - Prepare the correct amount of food and control portion sizes.
   - Offer for customers to take home their leftovers, and donate leftover ingredients to charities.

2) Reuse — use old products again for the same or a different purpose:
   - Glass bottles can be washed and refilled.
   - Containers can be reused for storage.
   - Some leftover food can be reused by caterers, e.g. leftover potatoes can be put in a salad.

3) Recycle — put materials that are recyclable into the correct bin:
   - Metals, glass, plastic, paper and card can all be recycled.
   - Businesses should use recycled or recyclable packaging.

Reuse this page by turning it into a paper plane...

... It might be worth reading it first though. A business looking to be more sustainable should tell their staff what their goals are. That way, everyone can work together to use fewer resources whilst doing their jobs.

Unit 1: Section 1 — Hospitality and Catering Provision

The Impact of Technology

New technology has a positive impact on the sector. It makes a lot of processes easier and faster.

Lots of Places take Cashless Payments

1) There are lots of ways that technology can be used to take payments:

> Contactless Payments — Most card readers take contactless payments, which means customers don't have to type in their PIN. This is faster and more convenient for customers.
>
> Website Payments — Lots of hotels allow guests to pay online when they book the hotel, or before check-out. In some restaurants and cafés, customers can scan a QR code, allowing them to pay for the bill on their phone. This relies on an Electronic Point of Sales (EPOS) system (see below).
>
> App payments — Customers might be able to download an app that lets them pay for their service.

2) Payments through a website or app remove the need for staff to be involved in taking payments. This means time can be spent on other jobs like serving people and cleaning the dining area.

3) Some places might choose only to take payments through a cashless system, which means they don't have to keep cash on the premises. This reduces the risk of theft and can lower insurance costs for the business.

Technology Benefits Customers and the Business

1) In some cafés and restaurants, customers can view the menu via an app, which saves on paper. They might also be able to make their order on the app, which can be more convenient for the customers and the business.

2) Lots of fast-food outlets have screens where customers can view the menu, order and pay. This reduces queues and makes the fast food even faster.

3) Some types of accommodation may allow for online or self-service check-in — this can speed up service and free up staff to carry out other necessary tasks.

4) Keycards for hotel rooms often use contactless technology. Some places can even put a guest's room key on an app.

5) Hotels might offer apps for things like booking activities, room service and dinner reservations.

6) As well as saving time for staff, apps can be a good way for hotels to advertise their other services.

Software can make Record-Keeping Easier

EPOS SYSTEMS
- These are machines and software that keep track of customers' orders.
- Machines are connected to a central computer. Staff put an order into one machine and it's sent to the computer, which records the order and creates the final bill.

STOCK CONTROL
- These systems monitor stock levels. When new stock comes in, it's added to the system to keep stock levels accurate.
- The system orders more stock automatically when levels fall.
- It stores information about the prices of stock too.

BOOKINGS
- This can record table or room bookings and stops the business from accidentally over-booking.
- It can help with planning staff shifts and dining room floor plans.

If only dinner with great aunt Mildred was contactless...

New technology will cost a business in the short term, but it can make processes much faster. In a restaurant, this means tables can be served faster, and serving more tables means more profit. So it's often worth the cost.

Unit 1: Section 1 — Hospitality and Catering Provision

The Impact of Media

Using media can help a business gain lots of customers, but it also risks them losing customers.

Different Types of Media can Promote Businesses

The hospitality and catering industry is very competitive, so it is important that establishments promote their business to gain customer awareness and stand out from their competitors. Businesses can use different forms of media to promote themselves:

Printed Media
This includes advertising in newspapers, magazines, leaflets and on billboards.

Broadcast
Businesses can pay to have scripted adverts played on television or the radio.

Internet
Businesses can create their own website or social media pages.
They can build brand awareness through travel websites, such as Tripadvisor.
They can also send out marketing emails, or advertise on podcasts.
Lots of businesses work with influencers — people who have a large following on social media. The business pays the influencer to post about them online, advertising the business to their followers.

Competition
Establishments can stand out from competitors by offering competitions, deals and discounts. They can also use media to stand out by having a user-friendly website, and by being easy to contact and quick to respond to messages from customers.

There are Advantages and Disadvantages of Using Media

Advantages	Disadvantages
• Can reach a lot of people, so can build brand awareness and trust. Can also help attract new customers who hadn't yet heard of the business. • Most types of media can be used to target specific groups, e.g. a family holiday resort can advertise in a magazine bought mainly by parents. • Social media can be used for free and can reach people very quickly. • Businesses can use feedback from online reviews to help to identify things that need improving.	• Frequent adverts are needed for the business to become a well-known, recognisable brand. This means printed media and broadcasting can become very expensive. • The number of people who watch live TV is decreasing, as people turn to streaming services that offer ad-free viewing options. • Building websites and an online presence can be costly. • Offering competitions and discounts could mean the business makes less profit.

Even if a business chooses not to use media themselves, they are often still affected by it. For example, customers can still post reviews about their experiences on social media or on third-party websites:
- Positive reviews on the internet can attract new guests and help the business stand out from competitors.
- Negative reviews can spread quickly. They can put guests off and decrease customer loyalty to the brand.

Businesses employ spiders to make their web-sites...
Social media is a popular affordable method of advertising in the hospitality and catering industry. But a business has less control over it's image if it uses social media compared to other forms of advertising.

Unit 1: Section 1 — Hospitality and Catering Provision

Revision Summary for Unit 1: Section 1

It's time to put yourself to the test to see how much you can remember about hospitality and catering provision.
- Tackle the summary questions below. Yes, they're hard — try to answer them from memory to really test how well you know the topic. The answers are all in the section, so go over anything you're unsure of again.
- When you've done all the questions for a topic and are completely happy with it, tick off the topic.

Commercial and Non-Commercial Provision (p.3-6)
1) Describe the difference between commercial and non-commercial provisions.
2) Give six examples of non-commercial establishments. For each example, state whether it is residential or non-residential, and give the main purpose of the establishment.
3) Briefly describe seven different types of commercial residential businesses.
4) Briefly describe seven different types of commercial non-residential provision.

Types of Food Service, Standards and Ratings (p.7-9)
5) Describe five different types of table service.
6) Give three types of counter service. For each type, give an example of an establishment that might use this style of service.
7) Outline some features that a hotel must have to achieve each of the five AA star ratings.
8) Write down four different awards and ratings given to food services and describe what each of them assesses.

Employment Roles, Qualifications and Experience (p.10-14)
9) Name six front of house roles. Give one responsibility and one useful attribute for each.
10) Describe four roles in housekeeping. What personal attributes would be good for a housekeeping role?
11) Describe the different roles in the kitchen brigade, from most senior to least senior.
12) Name three types of management role in hospitality and catering, and list their responsibilities.
13) What is an apprenticeship? Explain how it is different to work experience.
14) Give four examples of qualifications that some roles in hospitality and catering may require.

Contracts, Pay and Benefits (p.15-16)
15) Describe the different types of contract that can be offered to employees. Give one advantage and one disadvantage of each.
16) Explain the difference between a salary and a wage.
17) Describe five benefits that employers can give their workers.

Factors Affecting the Hospitality and Catering Provision (p.17-22)
18) Identify the three basic costs for a business and give three examples of each.
19) State the difference between gross profit and net profit.
20) What is value added tax (VAT)? Who pays VAT?
21) Explain how the value of the pound affects the hospitality and catering industry in the UK.
22) Give six steps that add to the carbon footprint of turning ingredients on a farm into a dish in a restaurant.
23) Explain why using local seasonal ingredients is more environmentally friendly than importing ingredients.
24) Give five ways that a hotel with a restaurant could reduce its energy and water use.
25) What are the three Rs in sustainability? Give an example of each.
26) Identify the benefits of cashless payments to a business.
27) How could a hotel use mobile apps to benefit their business?
28) Describe three types of software that a restaurant could use to improve their record-keeping.
29) Describe four types of media that businesses can use to promote themselves. Give one advantage and one disadvantage for each.

Unit 1: Section 1 — Hospitality and Catering Provision

Operational Requirements

This section is about how providers run their daily operations to satisfy customers. First, let's look at workflow.

Operations are Split into Front of House and Back of House

1) The parts of a hospitality business can be sorted into front of house and back of house:

   - Front of house means the customer-facing parts of the provider, such as the reception and dining areas — it's all the places a customer can go.
   - Back of house is all the parts of a business that don't directly deal with customers, including the catering kitchen, marketing (see p.13), or a hotel's housekeeping team (see p.11).

2) Both parts of the business need to have a good workflow to run smoothly.

3) Workflow is the series of activities that need to take place for a job to be completed. For example, in a catering kitchen, this is everything that needs to happen to prepare food for a customer.

Front of House Workflow is About Serving the Customer

1) The front of house works differently in residential and non-residential businesses.

2) In a non-residential business (e.g. a café or restaurant), the front of house workflow begins with customers entering the reception area.

3) The reception area will be different depending on the type of service (see p.7-8) offered by the business.

   - Most restaurants and some cafés offer table service — the front of house staff will need to direct customers to an available table. There may be a waiting area or bar for customers to use where they might be able to look at a menu or order drinks.
   - If the business offers counter service, then customers will usually seat themselves.
   - Some businesses may have no dining area and operate only as a takeaway.

4) As with residential businesses on the next page, it's important for the front of house to be welcoming — e.g. through nice decorations and music. It's also important to consider whether all areas are accessible for people with disabilities.

5) The dining area should be kept clean and comfortable and needs to be monitored by staff to make sure customers are being served. A large seating area might be divided up into different areas that each member of staff is responsible for.

6) The front of house needs to be laid out in a way that lets it run smoothly:

   - The staff need to be able to access the kitchen easily so they can serve food and clear away dirty plates, glasses, etc.
   - The staff also need to have easy access to extra equipment (such as sauces or extra cutlery).
   - In a more informal setting, like a cafeteria, customers might serve themselves and help with tidying away dirty equipment. The layout should make it easy for customers to see where everything is (or needs to go) and get what they need.

7) The business needs to take payment at some point in its workflow. For counter service, this usually happens at the point of ordering. For table service, a waiter usually takes payment at the end of the meal.

I used to run the counter service for NASA — Three, Two, One...

People would always give me weird looks when I served them dessert before anything else. Anyway, make sure you know what workflow is and how front of house workflow can change for different businesses.

Operational Requirements

The Front of House in Residential Businesses Checks People In

1) In a residential business (e.g. a hotel), the front of house is the first point of contact for customers.

2) The reception area should be welcoming and it should be clear to customers where they need to go when they enter the building.

3) Many businesses will have an area for customers to sit down while waiting to be served. In a hotel, this could be part of the bar area.

4) Receptionists need to check customers in, give them keys or key cards for their rooms and direct them to their accommodation. There needs to be good coordination between the front and back of house to ensure the right rooms are ready on time.

5) Many residential businesses also provide catering, e.g. a hotel might provide breakfast for its guests, or it could have a restaurant for both guests and other customers. The entrance to the catering area is usually shared with the residential part of the business.

Some residential businesses may have self-service check-in facilities, instead of a receptionist.

The Kitchen's Workflow is More Complicated

In the back of house, the workflow of the kitchen has several steps you need to know about. The purpose of the kitchen's workflow is to prepare food for customers as quickly as possible — but it also needs to do this safely.

1. Delivery
- The kitchen workflow starts with ingredients being delivered by suppliers.
- Ideally, this area will be close to where a delivery vehicle can stop.
- Staff handling deliveries might need some space to do quality checks and to keep records (see p.32). Also, some products may need washing before they are stored.

2. Storage area
- This should be close to the delivery area for convenience and so people don't pass through the food preparation areas while unloading.
- Different foods need to be stored in different ways — the storage area should have space to keep things chilled or frozen if needed.

3. Preparation and cooking area
- The main area of the kitchen is where food is removed from storage, prepared and cooked.
- This area needs space for all the necessary cooking appliances and utensils, as well as work surfaces. The appliances will need to be connected to a source of gas or electricity.

4. Serving area
- This area will have space for plating up food in places with table service.
- It needs to be accessible to the front of house staff serving customers.
- The area might have appliances to keep food hot or cold as needed while it is stored there.

5. Washing and cleaning area
- This area takes in dirty equipment from the kitchen and the front of house for washing-up.
- Cleaning can be done using dishwashers or by hand in sinks.

No joke here, sorry — thinking about hotel breakfasts is distracting...

The kitchen workflow might look difficult at first, but the order is pretty logical if you break it down into the stages above. Keep the order of these stages in mind when looking at kitchen layout on the next page.

Operational Requirements

Areas for Staff are Important

- Front and back of house staff need an area away from customers and the main kitchen where they can take a break and go to the toilet.
- A staffing area for kitchen staff should also have a place where they can change between outdoor clothes and clean clothes (e.g. their uniform) for working in the kitchen.
- There should be a wash area with sinks for handwashing at the points where staff cross in between the kitchen and staff areas.

Kitchen Layout is About Safety and Efficiency

1) The kitchen should be laid out in a way that helps its workflow — i.e. the layout should help with preparing food quickly and safely.

2) Commercial kitchens will be very different depending on the size of the establishment, the building they're in and what equipment they need, but kitchen layouts have some common features:

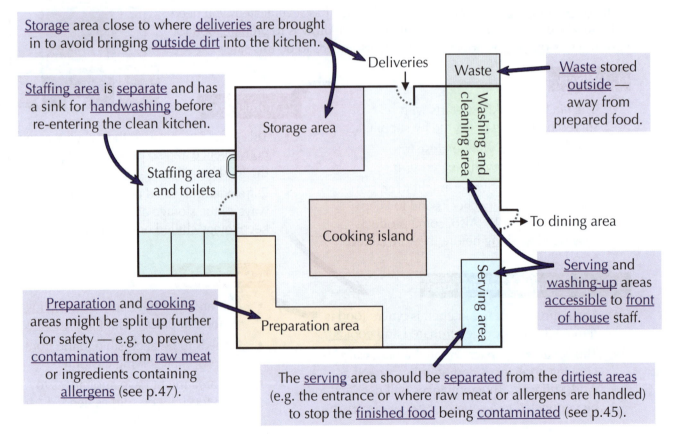

Storage area close to where deliveries are brought in to avoid bringing outside dirt into the kitchen.

Staffing area is separate and has a sink for handwashing before re-entering the clean kitchen.

Waste stored outside — away from prepared food.

Preparation and cooking areas might be split up further for safety — e.g. to prevent contamination from raw meat or ingredients containing allergens (see p.47).

Serving and washing-up areas accessible to front of house staff.

The serving area should be separated from the dirtiest areas (e.g. the entrance or where raw meat or allergens are handled) to stop the finished food being contaminated (see p.45).

3) This example helps the kitchen work smoothly as each stage is located near the ones before it and after it. For example, the storage area (step 2 on the previous page) is next to the delivery entrance (step 1) and the preparation and cooking areas (step 3).

4) Creating a layout where staff don't have to move around as much is also important for safety as it reduces the risks of tripping or bumping into someone carrying something hot.

Cooking Island sounds like a lovely place for a holiday...

The diagram above is just an example — commercial kitchens vary massively depending on what space is available to them. You need to know the key features that make the layout as safe and efficient as possible.

Unit 1: Section 2 — How Providers Operate

Equipment and Materials

Making meals for a lot of people is hard work, but catering kitchens have some special kit to help them.

Large Scale Equipment Helps with Serving Lots of People

1) The large scale, industrial pieces of equipment in a catering kitchen are quite different to what you normally find in a home kitchen.
2) They are usually fixed in place and run off electricity or gas (or sometimes both).
3) Large scale equipment can help with various tasks, for example:

Storage

Walk-in fridge-freezers can store a large amount of food and make it easy for kitchen staff to find what they need.

Glass chillers keep drinks in glass bottles or cans cool. They can also store clean glasses at a low temperature to help with serving cold drinks.

Preparation

Floor-standing food mixers can help with preparing large quantities of food, e.g. mixing cake batter, whisking cream or kneading dough.

Cooking

Catering kitchens often have large pieces of equipment for specific cooking tasks:

- A large conventional oven for baking or roasting.
- Deep fat fryers are used for deep frying, and steamers are used for steaming. (No surprises there...)
- Hot plates (sometimes called a griddle) are used to cook food from below with direct heat — e.g. for frying eggs.
- A standing bain-marie can be used to apply gentle heat (e.g. for melting chocolate), or to keep food warm until it is served.
- Hot water urns are useful for quickly making hot drinks to order.

Bains-marie are sometimes called water baths or double boilers.

Cleaning

- A pass-through dishwasher has racks that can be loaded up ready to go in as soon as the dishwasher is ready — this maximises the time that the dishwasher is cleaning things.
- Glass washers are specially designed for washing glasses — they use a lower temperature than dishwashers as glasses are more fragile.

Glass chiller — a greenhouse where you can go to relax...

Make sure you learn all the different large pieces of equipment on this page. It can also be helpful to have a picture in your head for each one to help you remember how they are used in the kitchen.

Unit 1: Section 2 — How Providers Operate

Equipment and Materials

Kitchens Also Need Lots of Small Equipment and Utensils

1) A catering kitchen doesn't just have a lot of large equipment — it also needs a large supply of smaller pieces of equipment, including utensils.

2) Utensils are handheld tools used for cooking, mixing and serving food, e.g. a chef's knife or a spatula.

3) Small equipment and utensils are different to large equipment in a few ways:

   - Small equipment is similar to what you'd use domestically (at home) — it's usually the same size and doesn't have a special name, unlike some large equipment.
   - It usually doesn't require gas or electricity to run (although some small equipment might be powered, e.g. an electric whisk or weighing scales).
   - Unlike large equipment (and what most people have at home), catering kitchens have lots of individual bits of small equipment.

4) Like large scale equipment, small equipment is used for various tasks, such as:

   Preparing food:
   e.g. chopping boards, measuring jugs, mixing bowls

   Cooking food:
   e.g. saucepans, baking tins and trays

   Serving customers:
   e.g. plates, bowls, cutlery

Businesses Need the Right Equipment to Create a Safe Environment

1) Like everything else in a kitchen, equipment needs to be kept clean for safety. Large equipment should be taken care of according to the manufacturer's instructions.

2) To keep everything clean, a business needs to have the right cleaning supplies, e.g. cleaning chemicals, cloths, mops and buckets. It also needs bins for disposing of waste — there might be several different ones to help recycle waste.

Gas and electric appliances should regularly undergo safety checks carried out by a professional.

3) It's important for the building to have the right number of fire extinguishers, smoke alarms and carbon monoxide detectors — and to make sure these are all working.

4) In addition to their dress code (see the next page), kitchen staff might need extra personal protective equipment (PPE). For example, oven gloves are worn when handling hot trays or dishes.

5) There should also be a first aid box that staff can easily use — it might be appropriate to have one each for the front and back of house. First aid boxes should contain:

   - Triangular bandages
   - Safety pins
   - Sterile eye pads
   - Unmedicated wound dressings
   - Individually-wrapped plasters in different sizes
   - Disposable gloves
   - Instructions on how to use these things

In a kitchen, blue plasters are used as they're easy to spot if they come off.

I was very unpopular when I ordered individually-wrapped pasta...

That's another page about equipment and materials done, and there's one more to go. Safety is a big part of a lot of these topics — e.g. a safe kitchen layout on page 26 and health and safety forms on page 32.

Unit 1: Section 2 — How Providers Operate

Equipment, Materials and Dress Code

Good Quality Equipment is a Good Investment

1) High quality equipment is expensive. The best pieces of large equipment can be very expensive, while small equipment often needs to be purchased in large quantities, so high individual prices (e.g. for top-of-the-range pots and pans) can add up too.

2) However, there are some key advantages to investing in high quality equipment:

- Having high quality equipment in the front of house creates a good impression for customers.
- High quality equipment should last longer and work more efficiently — over time, this will save the business money and will reduce the impact on the environment.
- Large pieces of equipment might have a warranty (the manufacturer will fix any problems that occur in the first few years).

Many Places Have a Dress Code for Staff

Front of house

1) Many businesses have a dress code for customer-facing staff in order to make a good impression and appear respectable and professional.

2) Some establishments provide a uniform for staff, and others may have a dress code. For example, a hotel might ask its reception staff to wear black and white business dress, and might have rules on the amount and type of jewellery that can be worn.

3) A business could also require its staff to make sure their clothes are clean and that they have good personal hygiene.

4) It should be clear to customers who the front of house staff are, so they know who to go to for assistance — uniforms and name badges can help with this.

Back of house

1) As they are in the back of house, dress codes for kitchen staff are more about safety than the impression made on customers.

2) The traditional chef's uniform is known as 'chef's whites'. However, it's not just worn because of tradition — some features of the uniform are important for safety:

- A head covering is worn to protect food from sweat and loose hair.
- To prevent injuries, shoes should not be slippy and should cover the whole foot.
- Aprons, long trousers and a double-breasted jacket with long sleeves are worn for protection against scalding from hot liquid splashing. Aprons are also easy to change if they get dirty.

3) Even if a kitchen doesn't require a uniform, back of house staff need to make sure their clothing meets these safety requirements. They should also make sure their clothing is clean and that they aren't wearing (or cover up) nail varnish, false nails or jewellery when working.

Due to tradition, I always wear ski goggles when cooking...

You might laugh, but I've never cried while chopping onions. It's important to know the different reasons behind dress codes in the front and back of house — whether it's about safety or making an impression.

Unit 1: Section 2 — How Providers Operate

Administration and Documents

Keeping a catering kitchen running smoothly can be pretty complicated — businesses need ways to keep track of what they've got and what they need.

Stock Control is Crucial for Running a Catering Business

1) Stock control is where a business keeps track of what stock it currently has, how much it has been using and what it needs to order.

2) Good stock control is really important to a catering business — to operate safely, it needs to make sure food is stored in the right way and is thrown away when it goes out of date.

3) Catering businesses also need good stock control to make sure they have what they need to meet customers' orders on a shift, but without buying so much stock that there is lots of waste.

4) A business might have to review whether its system is working well. For example, if it is ordering something very frequently, it might be able to save money by making bulk orders — this is fine as long as the food has a long enough shelf life and there's space to store it.

5) One method of stock control that's well suited to catering businesses is 'First In, First Out':

> **First In, First Out (FIFO):** A method of stock control where the oldest stock is always used up before any newer stock.

- This system helps businesses to reduce the amount of food that goes out of date while sitting in storage waiting to be used.

- This means there should be fewer health and safety risks, as well as less waste from throwing food away — which means less of the business's money wasted.

- To put this system into practice, when new stock is delivered it should go into storage at the back of the shelf, behind the older stock of the same type.

- If an ingredient is stored loose in a container, then containers of different ages shouldn't be mixed — otherwise it would be unclear when the food goes out of date.

6) Whatever method of stock control is used, businesses still need to check that ingredients haven't gone out of date before they are used. They also need to make sure their storage system is safe to help avoid contamination (see pages 48-49).

Stock Control Systems can be Computerised

1) Keeping track of how stock is used and deciding when to order it can be a complicated job — some businesses employ a dedicated administrator to help.

2) Electronic stock control systems can also be used to help with management.

3) The systems monitor how stock levels change over time and calculate how much stock is needed.

4) Some systems will order new stock automatically when levels fall.

The new stock control system hadn't made things simpler.

The best method of stock control for magic beans? Fee-FIFO-fum...

First In, First Out is a handy method of making sure things get used before they go out of date. Even better, it works exactly the way you'd expect based on the name. Don't you love it when that happens?

Administration and Documents

Businesses Need to Know How Much Stock They Have

1) In order to have a good stock control system, businesses need to keep track of how much they have in the first place.

2) To do this, they need to complete stock control forms:

Completed by:			
Date	Item	Quantity	Location

This is a very simple stock control form — it could also include things like the value of the items, or when they go out of date.

3) Stock control forms might also have spaces to say whether something needs to be reordered.

4) Unless the business has decided to stop buying something, if an ingredient runs out then more of it needs to be ordered. A good stock control system will help kitchens avoid running out of vital ingredients.

5) The system should show when something needs reordering so more arrives before it runs out. This can vary depending on the item — it depends on how quickly the amount is going down, how long it will take to deliver and how long it stays fresh for before it has to be thrown away.

There are Different Forms to Record Orders

1) When a business wants to place an order, they complete an ordering form to list everything they want from their supplier.

2) The supplier will send an invoice. This is like a bill — it shows what was bought and how much it will cost, and includes instructions on how to pay for it. The invoice could be sent physically with the delivery or it could be sent electronically.

3) When the stock is delivered, the supplier will provide a delivery note — this is another summary of what was in the order. The purchaser might need to sign the delivery note to say they've checked the delivery and accepted it.

4) These forms have quite a lot of features in common:

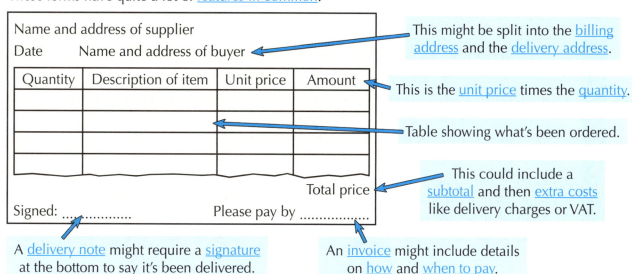

This might be split into the billing address and the delivery address.

This is the unit price times the quantity.

Table showing what's been ordered.

This could include a subtotal and then extra costs like delivery charges or VAT.

A delivery note might require a signature at the bottom to say it's been delivered.

An invoice might include details on how and when to pay.

Bad product idea #378 — 'I ♥ Admin' T-shirts...

These forms are all pretty similar — they all boil down to listing how much of each item there is in storage or in an order. Make sure you know the purposes of using ordering forms, bills and delivery notes.

Unit 1: Section 2 — How Providers Operate

Administration and Documents

Catering Providers Should Keep Records of Deliveries

- A catering business might have its own forms to fill in when accepting an order.
- Deliveries need to be checked before they are accepted — the catering provider should reject anything that's damaged to the point where it could have been contaminated, as well as anything beyond its 'use by' date.
- If the food has to be stored within a specific range of temperatures, it should be checked at delivery to make sure it's within this safe range (see p.50).
- Businesses often have written agreements with their suppliers that set out the reasons they can reject deliveries. Staff need to be trained to know what they are looking for when checking a delivery.
- It's useful to keep a record of the checks made — e.g. to see if certain problems keep happening. A form to fill in on delivery could look like this:

Delivery temperature was very important to Simone's Cones.

Date	Food	Supplier	'Use by' date	Temperature (°C)	Actions taken	Signature

There are also Documents for Health and Safety

Businesses are also required by health and safety laws to keep certain records.

Accident Forms

1) One example of this is an accident book — or separate accident forms. Businesses with over 10 employees have to keep an accident book, and all businesses have to report major injuries.

2) Accident forms are an important record that can help to determine if someone or something was at fault for an accident. Keeping a record of multiple accident forms could allow a pattern to be spotted that might be due to an underlying problem with the workplace. There's more about accident forms on p.41.

COSHH Forms

1) Another example of a health and safety document is a COSHH form. COSHH stands for 'Control Of Substances Hazardous to Health'.

2) If a substance (e.g. an ingredient or cleaning product) used in the kitchen is hazardous, it should have a COSHH form that lists the ways it could be harmful. For example, working with flour can produce a lot of flour dust in the air, which can cause people to develop asthma.

3) COSHH forms might also give details of procedures that should be followed to reduce the risk. E.g. in the flour example, one procedure would be to install and maintain a suitable ventilation system. If the COSHH form doesn't give these details, a risk assessment (see p.42) should be carried out to identify how to work safely.

There's more on COSHH and COSHH forms on p.39.

Bring a thermometer next time your food shopping gets delivered...

Making sure that a delivery is in good condition is really important to catering businesses — if they just accept it on the spot, they risk having to throw lots of food (and therefore money) away later.

Unit 1: Section 2 — How Providers Operate

Meeting Customer Needs

Hospitality and catering providers should do all they can to accommodate the needs of their customers.

There are Benefits to Meeting Customer Needs

1) Caring for customers means going above and beyond to meet their needs as best as possible.

2) There are lots of reasons why hospitality and catering businesses should put effort into caring for their customers:

- If customers think the service they received was good, they are much more likely to come back.
- It can be a free form of advertising, as happy customers may tell their friends about it, or post positive reviews online.
- It can help the business to stand out from its competitors.

Customer Rights are Part of the Law

1) Businesses must follow various laws in the UK that aim to protect customers.

2) Under the Equality Act (2010), businesses cannot discriminate against people based on certain protected characteristics. These include things like age, disability, race, gender and sexual orientation, as well as people's beliefs, such as their religion.

3) This means they must treat all customers equally. To ensure all customers experience the same service, the business may need to adapt parts of their service to suit the diverse needs of customers.

4) The business may need to provide extra facilities for some guests to make their experience easier. This includes people with disabilities, families with small children and people who are pregnant.

EXAMPLE

Businesses have to provide facilities and services to help guests with disabilities. There are lots of things that hospitality and catering providers can do to accommodate these needs:

- Provide Braille signs for blind people or audio induction loops for hearing-impaired people.
- Offer hotel rooms on the ground floor with disabled access and additional features such as handles and emergency cords.
- Parking spaces near the entrance can be reserved for customers with disabilities.
- Ramps or lifts can be installed to allow disabled access throughout the building.
- Staff should be patient and listen to customers so they understand what support is needed.

Sometimes, it might not be possible for a business to provide full disabled access, e.g. they might not be able to add a lift into an old or small building. But businesses should make adjustments where reasonable to make sure they're doing all they can to accommodate these guests.

5) Other laws aim to protect customers from harm or from businesses taking advantage of them. For example, under the Consumer Rights Act (2015) products have to be provided 'as described' (e.g. the description on a restaurant's menu should match the food it actually serves), and prices of services should be reasonable. Food safety laws also aim to protect customers (see p.51 for more).

Never in a trillion years have I exaggerated something on a menu...

The Equality Act applies to everyone in the workplace, not just customers. Employees must also be treated equally by their employer and colleagues. This helps create a friendly, welcoming environment.

Unit 1: Section 2 — How Providers Operate

Meeting Customer Needs

Customer Needs are Very Varied

1) Hospitality and catering businesses have to think about all sorts of possible customer needs. These will vary a lot depending on what the business is like, and who its customers are.

2) There are some essential customer needs that all establishments need to meet, for example:

- The service should be acceptable value for money (see page 36).
- The building should be accessible where reasonably possible, e.g. having lifts as well as stairs.
- The establishment should provide a clean and safe environment.

Customers have a range of needs and wants that they expect to be met. These might be essential, or they might be 'nice to have', e.g. having an iron in a hotel room.

Lifestyle can Impact Customer Needs

There are lots of lifestyle factors that can affect what customers look for from a hospitality or catering service:

1) Budget — the amount people are happy to spend depends on their disposable income. This varies a lot for different people, and it is also affected by the economy (see p.18). Businesses should keep up-to-date with the economic situation so they can try to set prices that are affordable, but still allow the business to make a profit.

2) Interest — any activities offered by a residential establishment should match with what their guests like to do in their spare time. E.g. a hotel specialising in family holidays could have a play area and a kid's club for children, and a golf course and relaxing spa for parents.

3) Eating patterns — families may want to eat dinner earlier than couples or guests on business. This will affect the opening hours of a catering establishment.

4) Time — some customers enjoy sitting down for a leisurely meal, whilst others prefer fast, casual dining options. Establishments should choose the correct type of food service (see p.7-8) to suit the majority of their guests. Large establishments could offer more than one type.

Dietary and Nutritional Needs are Important

- Dietary and nutritional requirements are covered in much more detail on pages 54-63, but they can have a big impact on customer needs.
- Catering establishments should have menus that are accurate and clearly labelled with foods that people may not be able to eat. This could be for health, religious or lifestyle reasons (see p.61-63).
- Customers might want to see extra nutritional information about the options on the menu. In the UK, larger businesses have to put the total number of calories in a dish on their menus.
- Waiting staff should ask guests if they have any allergies or dietary requirements before they take any orders, and listen carefully to their responses.
- They should also be knowledgeable about the ingredients in each dish so they can inform guests, and double-check with a chef if they are not sure — if a guest eats food they are allergic to, they can become dangerously ill (see p.47).
- Staff should put extra effort into catering for guests with dietary requirements, so the guest doesn't feel like they've missed out.

Oh, um, drat. I'm allergic to dishes over £10...

Eating patterns — making repeating shapes in your food...

Customers can sometimes have needs that are difficult to predict and prepare for. This is when it's really important for staff to listen to their needs and be proactive in finding a way to accommodate them.

Unit 1: Section 2 — How Providers Operate

Meeting Customer Needs

Needs Depend on the Type of Customer

- The needs of guests can vary depending on their reason for visiting a hospitality or catering provider.
- Businesses should think about possible needs of their guests and make sure they have the catering, equipment and accommodation resources to provide extra services if needed.
- Businesses should have a good idea of their target audience depending on the type of establishment they are (see pages 3-6), e.g. people travelling for work are unlikely to stay at a holiday park.

Leisure Customers

Guests may use facilities for celebrations, holidays or travel purposes.

1) Some guests look for a luxury experience whilst others want basic catering or accommodation that is value for money. Establishments can offer a range of options to cover more customer needs, or focus on one target audience.
2) Catering needs of leisure customers can include special dietary requirements, a children's menu option, and drinks and minibar facilities in accommodation.
3) For celebrating guests, restaurants and hotels offer special services, e.g. they might bring a cake out at the end of a meal, or offer a complimentary upgrade when they check-in to accommodation.
4) Some guests may require extra equipment such as high-chairs, cots or disability access (see p.33).

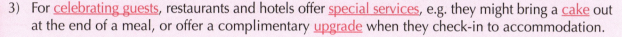

Business Customers

Some guests use hospitality facilities for work purposes such as conferences and training.

1) Guests travelling for work are likely to be busy — they might arrive late or need to leave early. Hotels can offer an early breakfast, 24-hour room service and express check-in and check-out to accommodate for this.
2) Some places have a designated 'quiet floor' for business guests, so they can work during their stay.
3) Rooms could be equipped with a trouser press or an iron and ironing board, so guests can press their work wear. They could also offer a laundry service.
4) Lots of establishments offer conference facilities — they need to provide all the equipment needed for conferences and meetings. Many places offer a catering service for conferences too.

Local Residents

Locals might use facilities but not stay overnight at accommodation.

1) Some hotels and holiday parks allow non-staying guests to use on-site leisure facilities like bars, restaurants, swimming pools and spas.
2) Establishments are likely to want to have a good relationship with local residents — their employees are usually locals too. They might try to keep noise to a minimum by closing bars at night, and provide parking for guests so they don't park near people's homes.

I just have one customer need — a pool with an inflatable flamingo...

As well as being able to give examples of different customer needs, you also need to have an idea of how a business might adapt to meet these needs. Such as having a pump to blow up your inflatable flamingo...

Unit 1: Section 2 — How Providers Operate

Customer Expectations

When booking a hotel or restaurant, the customer will have a level of service in mind that they expect to receive.

Expectations Come from Lots of Places

- Customers won't expect the same service from a fast-food restaurant as they'd get from a silver service restaurant. But they will have a certain standard of service in mind for each place they visit.
- It is important that a business meets its customer expectations, so that guests leave with a positive impression of the business.
- Their expectations come from a range of places that businesses need to be aware of:

Service and Value for Money

1) Guests expect the service from every hospitality and catering provider to be friendly and efficient.

2) They expect the level of service to match what they pay — it should be good value for money. This isn't the same as being cheap — a hotel could be expensive but customers will think it is worth it if the service they get during their stay is extra special.

3) Customers also have expectations about the product. For example, customers expect the food in a café to be tasty, nutritious and filling, and the price should feel reasonable for the quality.

Trends and Competitors

1) Customers expect businesses to keep up with trends in the industry, e.g. using current technology like mobile apps for orders and payments.

2) Businesses can look at what their competitors are doing to work out what trends they should follow. E.g. if a particular ingredient or style of cooking is popular with competitors, they should think about adding it to their menu.

3) Customers might expect something unique, so it can be good for businesses to stand out by offering new features that their competitors aren't, such as a distinctive theme.

4) Social media has a big influence on trends. This means that trends can change quite quickly, so businesses may need to make changes to their services regularly to stay competitive.

Clarence was great at adapting to the latest trends.

Media Influence

1) If customers have read reviews online, they will expect the service and products they receive to match what was described in the reviews.

2) It is important for businesses to be consistent and treat all customers equally (see p.33), so reviews are as accurate as possible.

3) Customers will also have expectations from any adverts they see or hear. Adverts should be accurate and honest so customers aren't disappointed.

Environmental Factors

1) Customers might expect a business to have environmentally friendly practices (see p.19-20).

2) They might expect dishes made with locally sourced, seasonal ingredients — a business could advertise this on their menu.

3) It can be useful for a business to look at what competitors are doing to be more sustainable.

Some hotels offer tennis lessons — their service is great value...

It's no good if a two-star hotel advertises that they offer five-star service — guests will be upset when they don't receive the service they expect. So businesses should be accurate and honest to control expectations.

Unit 1: Section 2 — How Providers Operate

Customer Demographics

Businesses should ask questions to find out what customers want and need from their service.

Market Research can Help Find a Target Audience

1) It can be very useful for hospitality and catering businesses to carry out market research.

2) This involves asking questions to the general public to get information about customer needs and their target audience — the group of people who are most likely to pay the business for its services.

3) Understanding their target audience can help businesses to:

- Identify the needs of their customers, so they can tailor their service to best suit their guests.
- Prepare any adaptations to their service that some guests may require.
- Identify who their competitors are.
- Find a unique selling point (USP) that appeals to guests and helps them stand out from competitors.

> A USP is something that a business offers as part of their service that none of their competitors offer. E.g. a hotel could be the only one in the local area that has spa facilities.

Knowing the Market Helps Businesses Meet Needs

1) Businesses should use market research to understand the market they're operating in, including its customer demographics.

2) Customer demographics are categories used to identify customers, such as age and income. Different demographic groups might be looking for different types of service.

3) There are lots of factors that can affect hospitality and catering businesses, for example:

Age
- Age can affect whether customers are looking for fast food or a luxury dining experience.
- Parents with small children are likely to want child-friendly facilities and a larger hotel room.
- Younger guests might be more interested in services that use up-to-date technology and keep up with trends.

Income
- People on high incomes are more likely to spend more on services, because a high price suggests it's of higher quality.
- People on low incomes are more likely to go for cheaper, budget options. E.g. they are more likely to opt for fast food than an expensive table service meal.

Location
- People travelling for work might look for accommodation and food in business areas.
- Accommodation and food services in quieter locations may suit older couples on holiday.
- Provisions near theme parks are likely to be popular with families.

Accessibility
- Customers will want parking if they have to travel by car to reach the establishment.
- Others may need good public transport links.
- Some customers may need specific accessibility features (see p.33).

Competition
- If customers have easy access to similar provisions in the area then competition will be high.
- The business can find out what customers do and don't like about these competitors.

USPs — Unexpected Saxophone Performances...

Everything on the last five pages is linked — businesses should have a good understanding of everything guests need and expect so their service is successful. Knowing customer demographics can help with this.

Unit 1: Section 2 — How Providers Operate

Revision Summary for Unit 1: Section 2

Hopefully you've optimised your workflow for this section on how providers operate — let's see if it's paid off.
- Tackle the summary questions below. Yes, they're hard — try to answer them from memory to really test how well you know the topic. The answers are all in the section, so go over anything you're unsure of again.
- When you've done all the questions for a topic and are completely happy with it, tick off the topic.

Operational Requirements (p.24-26)
1) What is workflow and why is it an important feature for businesses to think about?
2) Describe the front of house workflows in a restaurant and a hotel.
3) Describe each step of the workflow in a catering kitchen.
4) Give examples of staffing areas for front and back of house staff.
5) Explain how the following features of a kitchen layout help in preparing food quickly and safely:
   a) Storage area close to where deliveries are brought in.
   b) Serving and washing-up areas close to the door to the dining room.
   c) Preparation area split up from the cooking area.

Equipment, Materials and Dress Code (p.27-29)
6) List ten pieces of large scale equipment you might find in a catering kitchen and state what they are used for.
7) Give six examples of small equipment and utensils that a catering kitchen might need.
8) As well as a first aid box, identify what safety equipment a hospitality and catering businesses should have.
9) List seven items that first aid boxes should contain.
10) Give three advantages of investing in high-quality equipment.
11) Describe the key features of the front of house and back of house dress codes in a restaurant. Why are they different?

Administration and Documents (p.30-32)
12) Why is good stock control important for catering providers?
13) Explain what First In, First Out (FIFO) stock control is.
14) Describe how electronic systems can help with stock control.
15) Explain what businesses use each of the following forms for, and give three things that could be listed on each form:
   a) stock control form,   b) ordering form,   c) delivery note,   d) delivery check form.
16) Give two examples of health and safety documents and explain what they are used for.

Meeting Customer Needs (p.33-35)
17) Give three benefits to hospitality and catering businesses of meeting customer needs.
18) List four of the characteristics that the Equality Act (2010) states businesses cannot discriminate against.
19) How can hospitality and catering businesses accommodate the needs of people with disabilities?
20) Explain how businesses may adapt to satisfy lifestyle requirements and dietary needs of customers.
21) Explain the different needs of leisure customers, business customers and local residents.

Customer Expectations and Demographics (p.36-37)
22) Give examples of how a hotel and a restaurant could adapt their services to meet customer expectations in the following categories: a) service and value for money,   b) trends and competitors,   c) media influence,   d) environmental factors.
23) Explain how the age and income of customers affect the type of hospitality and catering services they look for.
24) Give three examples of how the location of an establishment affects its customer demographic.
25) How can an establishment use information on accessibility and competition to appeal to customers?

Health and Safety Laws

There are a number of health and safety laws that affect hospitality and catering establishments. They are put in place to minimise any risks that customers, employees and employers may face when on the premises.

The Workplace Must be Prepared for Hazards

1) The Health and Safety at Work Act (HASAWA) (1974) was created to protect people at work.

2) It gives rules that employers need to follow. Staff also have a responsibility to look after the health and safety of themselves and others.

Employer responsibilities:
- Ensure the workplace is safe, well lit and not too hot or too cold.
- Make sure workers are properly trained.
- Provide equipment that's safe to use.
- Create a fire policy.
- Make first aid available (see page 28).

Employee responsibilities:
- Put instructions learnt in training into practice.
- Use the correct safety equipment provided.
- Report fire and safety hazards to a manager.
- Report any accidents or injuries.

Hazardous Substances Must be Handled Safely

1) The Control of Substances Hazardous to Health Regulations (COSHH) (2002) are a set of rules for the handling of substances that can be dangerous to health, such as cleaning products, fumes and dust.

2) If not handled properly, they can cause health problems such as skin irritation, infections, asthma and cancer.

3) Hazard symbols are usually added to the COSHH form for a substance (see page 32) — they show the types of hazard that are associated with the substance. Some common hazard symbols are shown on the right.

4) One substance can have more than one hazard symbol, e.g. bleach is both corrosive and dangerous to the environment.

5) All staff must take action to put this law into practice to minimise the risk of health problems from these substances.

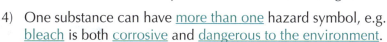
Irritant   Flammable   Corrosive

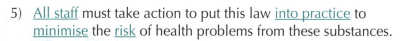
Environmental Hazard   Toxic

Employer responsibilities:
- Complete a risk assessment (see p.42) for dangerous substances.
- Provide correct storage. E.g. cleaning products should be kept in a locked cabinet and be clearly labelled.
- Provide training for employees, ensuring staff know what hazard symbols mean, and the actions to take when dealing with different hazardous substances.
- Provide suitable protective equipment, e.g. gloves and aprons.

Employee responsibilities:
- Attend COSHH training sessions.
- Only use substances that they have been trained to use.
- Follow instructions from training and use equipment provided when handling these substances.
- Make sure they understand the hazard symbols used on different substances.
- Wear protective equipment when working.

And there's also HTMTPCOT — how to make the perfect cup of tea...

For both HASAWA and COSHH laws, employers must supply the training and equipment that employees need to carry out their jobs safely. It is up to staff to put this into practice to keep everyone safe.

Health and Safety Laws

There are Safe Ways to Lift and Carry Things

- The Manual Handling Operations Regulations (1992) aim to reduce the risk of physical injuries from lifting and carrying heavy objects in the workplace.
- First, employers should see if there are any manual handling activities that could be avoided.
- They should store heavy equipment on the floor or on low shelves/worktops so it is easily accessible. If needed, they should provide carrying equipment such as a trolley or a forklift.
- Employers must run manual handling training and ensure that all employees who need it complete it.
- There is a correct way to lift and carry heavy objects:

   1) Assess the situation — check how heavy the object is and if there are other risks (e.g. if the object is hot or sharp, or the floor is uneven). If you don't think you're able to lift or carry something, ask for help.
   2) Lift — squat with feet either side of the object, keep your back straight as you lift and keep the object close to your body.
   3) Carry — the path should be clear and you should be able to see where you're going.

Staff May Need Personal Protective Equipment

1) Lots of risks can be avoided if workers wear the appropriate personal protective equipment (PPE).
2) This is addressed by the Personal Protective Equipment at Work Regulations (PPER) (1992).
3) Employers are responsible for assessing risks, providing PPE for staff and reminding them to wear it.
4) Staff should wear the PPE provided when necessary. This can protect others as well as themselves:

EXAMPLE

Kitchen staff should wear aprons, slip-resistant shoes, long sleeves and trousers (see p.29) — this protects them from hazards in the kitchen.

They may also have to tie hair back and wear a hair-net or hat, to stop them accidentally touching their hair and to stop loose hairs falling into food. This reduces the risk of contamination, which could cause harm to the customer (see p.45).

5) Other examples of PPE are masks, gloves and protective glasses.

Injuries and Dangerous Events Should be Reported

1) The Reporting of Injuries, Diseases and Dangerous Occurrences Regulations (RIDDOR) (2013) state that employers must record and report health and safety incidents to the Health and Safety Executive (HSE).
2) These are incidents which caused (or had the potential to cause) death, serious injury or disease.
3) Staff should let managers or employers know of any accidents or injuries that occur at work, such as slips, trips and falls from height. They should tell their employer if they are concerned about health and safety at work. If the employer does not take reasonable action, staff should go to the HSE.

Staff do a special elf and safety training course before Christmas...
For all of the laws and regulations on the last two pages, make sure you know what employers need to do and what employees need to do to make sure they are following the laws to keep each other safe.

Accident Forms

This page is all about how to fill in an accident form, with a lovely example for you to have a read of.

You Should Know How to Complete an Accident Form

1) If an accident happens in the workplace, an accident form must be completed. This helps to identify risks so that measures can be put in place to stop a similar accident from happening again.
2) Accident forms can look different, but they should all contain the same details about the incident.
3) A completed accident form should tell you what happened, when and where it happened, and who was involved. If someone was injured, it should also say what the injury was, what treatment was needed and when the employee returned to work.
4) Here is an example of a completed accident form:

Accident Form		
Date and time of accident: 5th January 2024 11:45 am	Location: Kitchen at Pomme de Terre	Name of injured person(s): Milly B. Clark (Sous chef)
Accident and injury details:	Slipped on spilt oil whilst carrying a pan of hot soup across the room. No injuries from falling but hot soup burnt Milly's left forearm.	
Details of First Aid provided (if any):	Burn was placed under cool water for 20 minutes. Antiseptic cream applied to burn. Left forearm was bandaged.	
When did/will employee return to work?:	Milly took the rest of the day off and decided she was fit to come into work the next day.	
What was the Hazard?:	Oil spillage on floor. Carrying pan of hot liquid across the kitchen.	
How could the accident have been prevented?:	Spillage should have been mopped up as soon as it happened or was noticed. Kitchen assistant usually responsible for cleaning floor, but they were off sick.	
Further action required?:	Consider improving kitchen layout to reduce the need for hot food to be carried a long way across the kitchen. Inform staff they are all responsible for cleaning up spills. Make sure kitchen assistant role is always covered.	
Signed:	J Bloggs JOE BLOGGS	

The injured person could be an employee, the employer or a visitor. In this case, it's an employee.

Description of the accident should be as detailed as possible. This helps identify the hazard.

Identifying what went wrong helps identify steps that can be taken to reduce risks.

Some of the larger actions (such as changing the layout of the kitchen) may not be carried out immediately, but should be considered if a similar accident happens again.

The form is signed by the person who filled it out. This could be any employee or the employer.

Joe had to fill out another accident form...

...he got a paper cut filling out Milly's accident form. Employers must keep a record of every accident that occurs in the workplace, and the more serious ones must be reported to HSE (see the previous page).

Risk Assessments

Unlike accident forms, risk assessments are completed to try to stop accidents from happening in the first place.

The HSE has a Five-Point Plan for Risk Assessments

- Risk assessment means thinking about possible hazards and making plans to minimise the associated risks.
- A hazard is something that can cause harm. Risk is the chance of a hazard causing harm.
- Risk assessment is used for both food hygiene and the safety of workers.
- The HSE (Health and Safety Executive) gives employers advice on how to do risk assessments. It has a five-point plan:

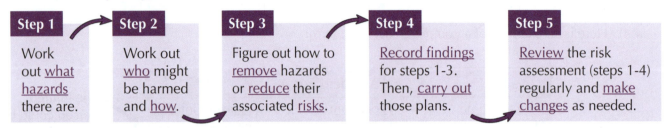

Step 1 Work out what hazards there are.

Step 2 Work out who might be harmed and how.

Step 3 Figure out how to remove hazards or reduce their associated risks.

Step 4 Record findings for steps 1-3. Then, carry out those plans.

Step 5 Review the risk assessment (steps 1-4) regularly and make changes as needed.

Risk Assessment Forms Show the Level of Risk

A risk assessment form should include all risks associated with working at the establishment. The example below is part of a complete form, filled out for one risk from working in the kitchen of a catering establishment:

Risk Assessment:		
Assessment carried out by: Suki Davies	Date of assessment: 05/01/24	Next review: 05/01/25
Hazards: Manual Handling — carrying heavy boxes of deliveries, sacks of flour, etc.	What is the risk?: Kitchen and waiting staff could suffer strains and bruising. LEVEL = MEDIUM	What control measures (actions) are needed?: Staff must have manual handling training. Buy smaller packs of goods where possible. Store heavy items on lowest shelves. Staff should work together to move heaviest items.
		Who must carry out the control measures?: Managers and Staff

Risks can be LOW, MEDIUM or HIGH. The level of risk depends on lots of factors, e.g. how heavy the delivery boxes are.

Businesses Need to Consider Risks to Everyone

Risk assessments should account for the risks to everyone involved in the business. This includes:

- Employees — e.g. kitchen staff may burn themselves on hot food or equipment.
- Employers may face the same health risks as employees if they also work hands-on in the business.
- Suppliers — e.g. people making deliveries could trip or slip while unloading.
- Customers — e.g. eating contaminated food could cause illness, or they may slip on a wet floor.

As well as risks to health like the ones in the box above, businesses also need to consider how to minimise risks to security. These risks include things like customers causing damage or harm by being violent, and loss of money or belongings from theft or fraud.

This book is a high-risk product — involuntary laughing may occur...
I wouldn't read it in a public place if I were you — you might get some funny looks. Remember that any employee can complete an accident form, but it's the employer who must carry out risk assessments.

Hazard Analysis and Critical Control Points

These next pages are about a process that catering establishments can use to identify and minimise food hazards.

HACCP is About Food Safety Hazards

- By law, catering businesses have to do a risk assessment (see previous page) for food hygiene.
- This is to stop food being contaminated before it reaches the customer.
- Food businesses in the UK must have a HACCP system:

Hazard Analysis and Critical Control Points (HACCP)

Analysis is when you look at something in detail.

A critical control point is a step in the process where possible hazards are reduced or removed to prevent harm to those who will eat the food.

- The HACCP system is used to control food hazards.
- A food hazard is something that makes food unsafe to eat — i.e. a person could become ill or be harmed if they eat it. There are three main types of food hazard:

  1) Physical — inedible material found in food, such as bits of plastic or metal.
  2) Chemical — chemical contamination of food, e.g. from cleaning products.
  3) Biological — contamination of food caused by living organisms or their products, e.g. harmful bacteria growing in food.

Rita insisted she was a very hygienic chef...

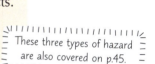

These three types of hazard are also covered on p.45.

There is a Correct Process for HACCP

- Catering establishments must keep a record of any HACCP assessments they carry out.
- They should come back to these records regularly to make sure the critical control points they put in place are working.
- The steps in the table below show how to carry out a HACCP assessment so nothing gets missed, and records are clear and easy to refer back to. There's an example of how to use these steps too:

HACCP Process Step	Example of Step (Reheating Food)
1) Identify hazards that must be controlled.	If food is reheated, bacteria could survive on the food. This is a biological hazard.
2) Identify the critical control points (CCPs).	The CCP is the thorough reheating of the food to kill bacteria.
3) Set limits for the CCPs.	Food must be reheated to at least 75 °C for the amount of time needed to kill the bacteria.
4) Monitor the CCPs.	Use a food probe to monitor the core temperature of the food. It must be at least 75 °C.
5) Take action if there is a problem.	E.g. ensure the kitchen has enough food probes and that staff know how to use them correctly.

- Employers must make sure that all members of staff follow the procedures identified from HACCP.

The chips looked dangerous — I ate them to control the hazard...

Safe to say the head chef didn't seem too pleased. Anyway, there are lots of new ideas on this page that may seem tricky at first. There's a handy table on the next page that'll hopefully make things a bit clearer...

Unit 1: Section 3 — Health & Safety

Hazard Analysis and Critical Control Points

There are Hazards in Every Step of Making a Dish

1) Food goes through lots of different steps before it's eaten by the customer.
2) Caterers need to think about the food hazards at every step and the control points that can reduce or remove them.
3) Here's an example HACCP table — there are three columns that must be filled in:

Ben was determined to reach the right temperature for reheating.

Step	Possible Hazard	Control Points for Hazard Prevention
Buying and receiving food	Food could be contaminated with bacteria if packaging has been damaged or if it's not been kept at the right temperature.	Buy from suppliers with a good reputation and refuse items that are not up to standard. Check the food is good quality, at the correct temperature and within its use-by date.
Storing food	Bacteria could grow on high-risk foods.	Store high-risk food in a fridge or freezer and record their temperatures regularly. Use a FIFO stock rotation system (see page 30).
Storing food	Bacteria could contaminate other foods.	Store raw meat away from cooked meat and from raw foods like salad or fruit.
Preparing food	Food could be contaminated with bacteria from staff, equipment or other food.	Staff should have good personal hygiene. Cooking equipment and surfaces should be kept clean. Use colour-coded chopping boards.
Cooking food	Bacteria could survive being cooked.	Food should be cooked to over 75 °C.
Cooling food	Bacteria that survive cooking could multiply. Bacteria could make toxins — substances that are toxic to humans.	Cool food within 90 minutes so it spends as little time as possible at the temperatures where bacteria can grow quickly.
Cooling food	Food could be contaminated by bacteria in the air or by things such as hair or dust.	Keep food covered while it's cooling. Staff should wear hats or hairnets. The kitchen should be kept clean.
Hot-holding food	Bacteria that survive cooking could multiply.	Keep hot-held food over 63 °C. Hot-hold food for a maximum of 2 hours.
Reheating food	Bacteria could survive being reheated.	Reheat food to over 75 °C.
Serving food	Bacteria could multiply. Bacteria could make toxins.	Serve food quickly to keep it out of the temperatures where bacteria can grow rapidly.
Serving food	Food could be contaminated from servers.	Servers should have good personal hygiene and make sure they don't touch the food. Their hair should be tied back.

There's more about the safe temperatures to store and cook food on page 50.

Bacteria can cause illness through food poisoning — see page 47.

HACCP, HACCP — sorry, all this excitement has given me hiccups...

If you haven't realised by now, health and safety in the workplace is really important. All these forms might seem boring, but they are a legal requirement for all hospitality and catering providers.

Unit 1: Section 3 — Health & Safety

Food Hazards and Symptoms

If you eat food that's contaminated you could become very ill — there are a number of ways this can happen.

Food Hazards Make Food Unsafe or Unfit to Eat

Food hazards are substances found in food that can cause harm or illness if eaten. There are four main types:

There's more on these types of food hazards over the next few pages.

Chemical contamination

Sometimes chemicals accidently contaminate food. These might be dangerous substances (such as toxic metals, cleaning products and pesticides) or toxins (poisonous substances). But they might also be 'safe' chemicals that were unintentionally added in excess, such as vitamins, preservatives or food colourings.

Physical contamination

Physical contamination is when objects are found in food that can cause harm, such as injury to the mouth, throat and stomach, damage to teeth, or choking. These can be found naturally in food (e.g. pips and bones), or could have been added unnaturally (e.g. plastic, glass and fingernails).

Biological contamination

Microorganisms such as bacteria can contaminate food. This can lead to food spoilage — signs of this include food turning slimy, sour-smelling or mouldy, but sometimes there are no obvious signs. Bacterial contamination can cause food poisoning (see p.47). Sometimes the bacteria affect the digestive system directly, and sometimes it's the substances they produce, e.g. toxins, that cause harm.

Allergies and intolerances

Food allergies and intolerances occur when substances that are harmless to most people cause a person to become unwell when eaten (see p.46-47).

Food-Induced Health Problems have a Variety of Symptoms

1) All types of food hazard can lead to visible and non-visible symptoms. Visible symptoms are those that you can see and, you guessed it, non-visible symptoms are those that you can't see.

   VISIBLE SYMPTOMS
   - anaphylactic shock
   - bloating
   - breathing difficulties
   - chills
   - diarrhoea
   - facial swelling
   - pale or sweating skin
   - rash
   - vomiting
   - weight loss

   There's more on anaphylactic shock on p.47.

   NON-VISIBLE SYMPTOMS
   - constipation
   - feeling sick
   - painful joints
   - stomach ache
   - weakness
   - wind/flatulence

2) Vomiting, diarrhoea and stomach pains are common symptoms associated with food-induced ill-health, particularly food poisoning (see p.47). But the symptoms experienced will vary depending on the food hazard consumed, as you'll see over the next couple of pages.

Revision allergy symptoms: procrastination, napping and snacking...

Harm from these food hazards is often caused by poor handling of foods — by law, businesses must have control measures in place to prevent this from happening. There's more on this later in the section.

Food Intolerances

Food intolerances often occur when someone can't digest a type of food properly, or the food causes irritation to the digestive system. Unsurprisingly, these can cause unpleasant symptoms.

People with Intolerances Must Avoid Certain Foods

1) Some people are intolerant to particular ingredients in food.
2) Eating the food can lead to illness, often affecting the digestive system.
3) People with food intolerances can experience a range of symptoms, such as bloating, vomiting, and stomach ache.
4) Although the intolerance can cause a person to feel very unwell, unlike allergies (see next page), its effects are not life threatening.
5) People with intolerances can sometimes eat small amounts of the food that they are intolerant to without having any symptoms.
6) Common intolerances are lactose, gluten, MSG and aspartame.

Unlike allergies, intolerances are not caused by an immune system reaction.

Lactose intolerance

- Lactose intolerant people can't easily digest lactose (a sugar in milk).
- They usually avoid things such as animal milk and dairy products. They often use soya drink or rice drink instead of animal milk.
- Symptoms of lactose intolerance include bloating, stomach ache, flatulence and diarrhoea.

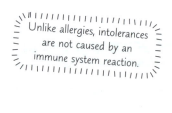

Gluten intolerance

- People with gluten intolerance can't digest a protein called gluten.
- Gluten is found in wheat and other grains, such as rye.
- Foods that normally contain gluten include flour, bread, cereals, pasta and sauces.
- Symptoms of gluten intolerance include stomach ache, feeling tired, bloating, diarrhoea, joint pain and vomiting.

MSG

- MSG is a natural salt that can be added to food as a flavour enhancer.
- People can experience symptoms of food intolerance when consuming lots of food containing MSG, such as headaches, sweating, feeling sick and weakness.

Aspartame

- Aspartame is an artificial sweetener that is added to food products such as diet soft drinks and sugar-free gum.
- Aspartame is one of the foods that individuals with the condition PKU need to avoid eating as it can cause brain damage, especially in babies and young children.

Snails, snakes, dolphins — all of them lactose...

Make sure you know the differences between food intolerances and food allergies on the next page. They're similar, but they aren't the same thing and it's important not to mix them up in the exam.

Unit 1: Section 4 — Food Safety

Food Allergies and Food Poisoning

If you've ever wondered why that dodgy kebab made you feel ill (just me?), then look no further...

Allergic Reactions can be Dangerous

1) Food allergies are caused by the immune system reacting to something in food.
2) Something that causes an allergic reaction is called an allergen. Common allergens include:
3) Allergic reactions can affect different organs and lead to symptoms such as a rash, vomiting, facial swelling, difficulty breathing, feeling sick and stomach ache.
4) A severe allergic reaction is called anaphylaxis, which can lead to anaphylactic shock (a complication of the reaction). This can lead to death and so medical treatment is needed immediately.
5) Even eating just a small amount of an allergen can cause a person with that allergy to have a severe reaction. This means it's important that food is properly labelled so that people with allergies know what they can safely eat (see p.51).

- cereals containing gluten (e.g. wheat)
- fruits and veg
- celery
- milk (dairy products)
- molluscs (e.g. mussels)
- crustaceans (e.g. prawns)
- sulphur dioxide and sulphites
- eggs
- tree nuts
- peanuts
- sesame seeds
- lupin
- soya
- fish
- mustard

Remember these Main Types of Bacteria

1) Food poisoning is an illness caused by food contaminated with bacteria.
2) Foods more likely to cause food poisoning are called high-risk foods, e.g. poultry and dairy products.
3) You need to know the following examples of bacteria that lead to food poisoning:

Bacteria:	Found in:	Symptoms include:
Bacillus cereus	reheated rice and other starchy foods, e.g. pastries and pasta	stomach ache, feeling sick, vomiting, diarrhoea, fever
Campylobacter	raw or undercooked poultry, other raw meats, untreated milk/water	stomach ache, diarrhoea, fever, feeling sick, vomiting
Clostridium perfringens	beef, pork, poultry, gravies	stomach ache, diarrhoea
Salmonella	raw poultry, untreated milk, eggs	stomach ache, diarrhoea, fever, feeling sick, vomiting
Staphylococcus aureus	human skin, nose and mouth — it gets onto food when people touch it	stomach ache, feeling sick, vomiting, diarrhoea, chills
Listeria	soft cheeses, pâté, shellfish	flu-like symptoms, e.g. fever, muscle ache, fatigue
E. coli	raw meat (e.g. beef mince), contaminated water, unwashed raw vegetables	stomach ache, diarrhoea, vomiting, fever, sometimes kidney damage

Pregnant women are at a higher risk of Listeria infection, and it can lead to miscarriage or health problems in the child.

Ylobacter — not a camp you want to pitch your tent at...

There are some big, scary names for these bacteria — make sure you know how to spell them (it took me a good 10 minutes to spell ~~Staffylowcouscous~~ Staphylococcus aureus) and the key facts about each.

Preventing Food-Induced Ill-Health

As we've seen so far in this section, if people eat contaminated food they could become very ill. That's why it's mega important that you handle food safely and hygienically to prevent bacteria spreading around the kitchen.

Bacteria are Transferred to Foods by Cross-Contamination

1) When working with food, it's really easy to pass bacteria from raw food to work surfaces, equipment and your hands. Bacteria are then easily transferred to high-risk food (food that is ready-to-eat, like cooked eggs and fish) — this is called cross-contamination.

2) There are different sources of cross-contamination, and steps must be taken to avoid it happening...

Food can be Cross-Contaminated by Other Foods

1) If a contaminated food comes into contact with other food, it can spread the contamination.

2) For example, raw meat juices can drip onto cooked food. High-risk foods such as gravy can contaminate lower risk foods when added to a meal. Soil containing bacteria on unwashed fruits and vegetables can contaminate other foods.

> Look out for signs of spoilage — it shows contamination has occurred, and the spoiled food could contaminate other food. It's good to find the cause of spoilage so control measures can be put in place to prevent it.

3) You can help prevent cross-contamination by:

- Keeping raw foods and cooked foods separate. Covering high-risk foods or storing them in containers to prevent cross-contamination, including in the fridge.
- Always storing raw meat, poultry and fish on the bottom shelf in the fridge to stop blood and juices dripping onto other food.
- Washing raw fruit and vegetables thoroughly when preparing dishes.
- Using a FIFO (First In First Out system) (see p.30) so that the oldest food (the first in) is used first. Regularly checking 'use-by' and 'best before' dates. Throwing away foods past their use-by date.
- Checking that waste bins are not overfilled and removing waste from kitchen areas.

Everything in a Kitchen must be Kept Clean

1) It's not just other foods that can cause cross-contamination, bacteria can be transferred from unclean work surfaces, utensils and equipment.

2) To help reduce the chance of cross-contamination, you can:

- Use coloured knives and chopping boards to prepare different food groups, e.g. you could use red for raw meat and green for salad and fruit.
- Use different utensils to serve different foods.
- Use clean equipment.
- Use a cleaning schedule so that equipment, floors and surfaces are cleaned regularly. This should include toilets and storage areas.
- Use an antibacterial spray to sanitise work surfaces.

I wouldn't cross with contamination if I were you...

It's dead easy for cross-contamination to happen. You have to be very careful and hygienic in the kitchen — especially if you're dealing with high-risk foods that bacteria just lurrrveee.

Unit 1: Section 4 — Food Safety

Preventing Food-Induced Ill-Health

People can be a Source of Cross-Contamination Too

1) Cross-contamination can be caused by people too.
2) This usually happens because of poor personal hygiene (especially unclean hands), as well as handling food when unwell. To help prevent it, food handlers should:

- Follow personal hygiene procedures. Hands should be washed, especially before and after handling high-risk foods, as well as after going to the toilet, sneezing or handling waste.
- Wear correct, clean uniform (see p.29) and PPE (see p.40).
- Cover any cuts with clean plasters.
- Make sure they're fit for work and report to the person in charge if they're ill.

Control Measures can Prevent Physical Contamination

1) Sources of physical contamination (see p.45) include:

- Materials from broken/damaged equipment, e.g. broken glass.
- Packaging / other materials, e.g. plastic, tin foil, plasters.
- Humans, e.g. hair and fingernails.
- Pests, e.g. flies and insects.
- Food, e.g. pips, seeds, bones, soil on unwashed fruits and vegetables.

Keep an eye out for signs that staff or the premises are unclean or untidy — it shows there's a risk of contamination.

2) To help prevent physical contamination, you can:

- Keep all areas clean and tidy. Clear up any breakages and throw all waste away immediately.
- Check food packaging for damage to prevent anything getting in, and keep food covered when it's not being used.
- Check equipment for damage and faults — report anything found and replace where necessary.
- Ensure all staff are wearing appropriate PPE. Wear hairnets or hats to prevent contamination with hair. Nail varnish, false nails and jewellery should not be worn when handling food. Use blue plasters so that they're easily spotted if they fall off.
- Store all personal belongings in staff lockers.
- Put control measures in place to stop contamination with pests.

To control pests, you need to stop access, e.g. installing fly screens and filling cracks in walls and floors. You should also remove the attraction, e.g. by keeping the premises clean and making sure food is inaccessible.

Chemical Contamination can be Prevented Too

1) To avoid chemical contamination (see p.45), people handling food should be careful not to add excess food additives, such as food colourings.
2) Chemicals, such as cleaning products, should be stored away from food areas. They should also not be overused when cleaning.
3) Businesses should follow COSHH guidelines (see pages 32 and 39).
4) Catering establishments should only purchase foods through reputable suppliers — some farmers may overuse pesticides or fertilisers, which may contaminate foods.

"Waiter, there's a fly in my soup." "Sorry sir, I'll get the fly spray."
Remember the HACCP system from pages 43-44? All of the things we've covered on the last two pages, are critical control points that you'd need to consider, so make sure you know them inside and out.

Unit 1: Section 4 — Food Safety

Preventing Food-Induced Ill-Health

We've already seen the consequences of consuming bacteria, so let's see how to prevent it from happening.

Microorganisms Grow in the Right Conditions

Bacteria need five conditions to quickly grow and multiply:

| warm temperature | plenty of moisture | plenty of food | the right pH | enough time |

High-risk foods are high in protein, which bacteria can use as food, and moist.
So if high-risk foods are not stored correctly, they can easily grow harmful bacteria.

The Right Temperature is Vital to Storing Food Safely

1) To preserve food, you need to keep it in conditions that bacteria can't grow in. A key factor that needs to be controlled is temperature. Here are some critical temperatures that affect bacterial growth:

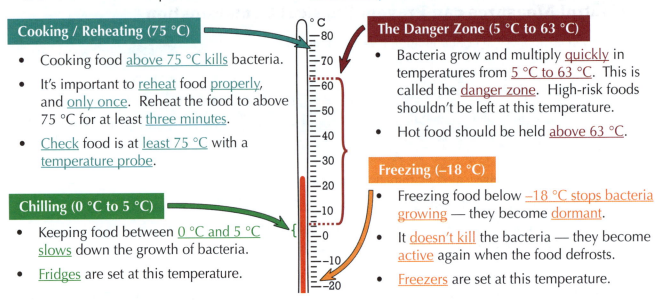

Cooking / Reheating (75 °C)
- Cooking food above 75 °C kills bacteria.
- It's important to reheat food properly, and only once. Reheat the food to above 75 °C for at least three minutes.
- Check food is at least 75 °C with a temperature probe.

Chilling (0 °C to 5 °C)
- Keeping food between 0 °C and 5 °C slows down the growth of bacteria.
- Fridges are set at this temperature.

The Danger Zone (5 °C to 63 °C)
- Bacteria grow and multiply quickly in temperatures from 5 °C to 63 °C. This is called the danger zone. High-risk foods shouldn't be left at this temperature.
- Hot food should be held above 63 °C.

Freezing (–18 °C)
- Freezing food below –18 °C stops bacteria growing — they become dormant.
- It doesn't kill the bacteria — they become active again when the food defrosts.
- Freezers are set at this temperature.

2) Temperature of food needs to be considered at each stage, from delivery all the way to serving:

Delivery	• Foods should be checked at delivery. High-risk foods should be rejected if refrigerated foods are above 5 °C or if frozen foods are warmer than –18 °C.
Storage	• High-risk foods should be stored in the fridge or freezer at the safe temperatures.
Preparing	• Defrost frozen food fully, in the bottom of a fridge and away from other food.
Cooking	• Cook food at the right temperatures and for the correct time. • Make sure food is cooked all the way through — e.g. cook thicker pieces of meat for longer than thin ones. • Test the core temperature inside food using a clean temperature probe. Different meats have different safe minimum core temperatures that must be reached.
Serving	• Serve hot food straight away or keep it above 63 °C for no longer than 2 hours. • If you're serving food cold or storing it, cool it down within 90 minutes.

Frying through the danger zone...

Temperature control is really important, so fridges and freezers with temperature displays should be checked daily to make sure they are working properly and keeping food at safe temperatures.

Catering and the Law

Food labels can help people make informed choices about what they eat. There are tonnes of rules about what must appear on food labels and these are set by UK laws.

Catering Businesses Must Follow Food Safety Laws

Food safety laws are set out to protect both businesses and consumers.

Food Safety Act

The Food Safety Act (1990) is a law.
It says all catering establishments must:
- make sure their food is safe to eat.
- check that any information given to customers about their food (e.g. on labelling) is correct.
- make sure the quality and composition of their food is what the customer expects.

The Food Safety and Hygiene Regulations

The Food Safety and Hygiene (England) Regulations (2013) ensure that food is always handled safely and hygienically from source to plate, following the HACCP system (see pages 43-44). There are similar laws that cover the rest of the UK.

Labels Must Tell You Certain Information by Law

1) For most of the UK, the FSA (Food Standards Agency) regulates food labelling laws and makes sure they're followed.

2) The law says that the following should be shown on food packaging:

Food labels must be clear, correct and not misleading.

- How to store the product.
- The product name and what it is (if the name doesn't make it obvious).
- The name and address of the manufacturer.
- A use-by date for high-risk foods or a best before date for other foods.
- The country it comes from if the buyer might be confused.
- Cooking and usage instructions.

- Most food labels have to show the weight, volume or quantity of the product, not including the packaging.
- The nutritional information of the product.
- All ingredients should be listed, so those with dietary requirements can check if they can eat the product.
- Common allergens should be clearly highlighted.
- Any genetically modified ingredients in the product should be listed.
- Ingredients must be listed in descending order of weight. There are certain ingredients where the quantity must be shown.

This page is best served chilled. Use by date: exam day...

Eating a certain food when you've got an allergy or intolerance to it can have very bad consequences, so it's super important for food packaging to list all of the ingredients to avoid them being eaten by mistake.

Unit 1: Section 4 — Food Safety

Role of the EHO

Just because there are protocols and laws in place to protect customers from food-induced health problems, doesn't mean they are always followed well. This is where Environmental Health Officers come in.

EHOs Enforce Laws Relating to Food Safety

1) An Environmental Health Officer (EHO) is an official employed by local authorities in the UK to protect the health and safety of the general public. In the hospitality and catering sector, they are responsible for ensuring businesses are obeying laws such as the Food Safety Act (see previous page).

2) They are allowed by law to inspect a catering establishment at any time without an appointment.

3) Businesses are inspected when they first open. Inspections may also happen following complaints made against the business, accidents at work, or outbreaks of pests, infectious disease or food poisoning to identify the cause and protect customers from harm.

EHOs Collect Evidence During Inspections

1) During an inspection, the EHOs check:

The food handlers
- Food handlers must have good personal hygiene and follow health and safety guidelines when handling food, including wearing appropriate PPE (see p.40).
- All food handlers must have completed necessary training and should have up-to-date certificates.

The food premises
- Premises should be maintained so that they are in good condition, clean and safe for both staff and customers.
- Equipment must be safe to use.
- Mandatory health and safety signs and posters must be displayed.

The working practices
- Food is safe to eat, is labelled correctly and is stored appropriately.
- Food is held at safe temperatures (see p.50) at all times, including when storing, cooking, cooling, freezing, displaying and serving food.
- A HACCP plan (see page 43) is in place to identify any hazards and risks, and to put control measures in place, including for preventing all types of contamination.

2) As part of their role, the EHO is allowed to collect evidence during an inspection.

3) Types of evidence include taking photographs, collecting samples to test for harmful bacteria, and conducting interviews with staff. They can also check record books that keep track of things like employee training and refrigerator and freezer temperatures.

Records? I can hold 27 eggs in one hand.

Poor Performance in Inspections has Consequences

1) Following the inspection, EHOs advise catering establishments to help them improve their hygiene. They can set a time frame for improvements to be made by, which they will check at a reinspection.

2) They can also close the business if the risk to the public is high, impose fines, or take legal action against catering businesses that break the law. They may need to give evidence in court in such cases.

3) After the inspection has taken place, EHOs also give the business a food hygiene rating (see p.9).

I'm just collecting this sample of doughnut for, erm, evidence...

Receiving a low food hygiene rating might not seem like such a big deal compared to fines or legal action, but having a poor reputation can lead to fewer customers, and this can lead to lower profits. Not good.

Unit 1: Section 4 — Food Safety

Revision Summary for Unit 1: Sections 3 & 4

We've made it through all things health and safety — now let's see how much you really remember.
- Tackle the summary questions below. Yes, they're hard — try to answer them from memory to really test how well you know the topic. The answers are all in the section, so go over anything you're unsure of again.
- When you've done all the questions for a topic and are completely happy with it, tick off the topic.

Health and Safety Laws (p.39-40)

1) Describe the responsibilities of employers and employees set out by the Health and Safety at Work Act.
2) What is a hazard symbol? Explain why hazard symbols are added to COSHH forms.
3) Outline the responsibilities of employers set out by COSHH. What about the responsibilities of employees?
4) What do the Manual Handling Operations Regulations (1992) set out to do?
5) Describe the importance of personal protective equipment (PPE) and give three examples of PPE that food handlers may wear.
6) Explain when an employee might go to the Health and Safety Executive.

Accident Forms, Risk Assessments and HACCPs (p.41-44)

7) Describe all of the details you should find on an accident form.
8) Describe the five-point plan for doing risk assessments given by the Health and Safety Executive.
9) Give four things that you'd find on a risk assessment form.
10) List four groups of people that businesses must consider when doing a risk assessment.
11) What is a critical control point (CCP)? Outline the HACCP process, including an example for each step.
12) Give an example of a possible hazard and CCP for each of the following steps of making a dish:
    a) buying and receiving food, b) storing food, c) cooling food, d) hot-holding food, e) serving food.

Food Hazards and Food-Induced Ill-Health (p.45-47)

13) State what a food hazard is and describe the four main types of food hazard.
14) Give six examples of visible symptoms and six examples of non-visible symptoms caused by food hazards.
15) Explain what a food intolerance is.
16) Describe four examples of common food intolerances.
17) What is an allergen? Name five common examples.
18) Explain why people with food allergies should be careful not to eat any foods containing the allergen.
19) Name seven bacteria that cause food poisoning.
    For each type of bacteria, name one common source of the bacteria and one symptom caused by it.

Preventing Food-Induced Ill-Health (p.48-50)

20) What is cross-contamination?
21) Describe how cross-contamination from other foods can be prevented in a kitchen.
22) Give five ways that you can reduce the chance of cross-contamination caused by unclean work surfaces, utensils and equipment.
23) Describe what food handlers can do to prevent cross-contamination caused by people.
24) Give three ways to prevent physical contamination. Now do the same for chemical contamination.
25) Give the critical temperatures required for cooking, chilling and freezing food.
    Why are these temperatures important?
26) Describe the precautions taken to keep food at safe temperatures from the point of delivery to serving.

Catering Laws and the Environmental Health Officer (p.51-52)

27) Explain the aims of the Food Safety Act (1990) and the Food Safety and Hygiene Regulations (2013).
28) Describe everything that food labels must show on food packaging by law.
29) Describe the role of an Environmental Health Officer (EHO) and what they check during inspections.
30) What can an EHO do if a business performs poorly during an inspection?

Unit 2: Section 1 — The Importance of Nutrition

Nutrients and Fats

There are seven main nutrients you need for a healthy diet, and luckily for you, this section covers them all...

The Body Needs Macro-Nutrients and Micro-Nutrients

1) Fats, proteins and carbohydrates are macro-nutrients. 'Macro' means large, and funnily enough our bodies need these macro-nutrients in large amounts. Fats, proteins and carbohydrates are macro-nutrients that provide energy.

2) Dietary fibre and water are also macro-nutrients. These do not provide energy.

3) Vitamins and minerals are all micro-nutrients — we need them in small amounts. They are used in processes that keep us alive and well.

You'll find out more about all of these nutrients over the next few pages.

Fats Provide Energy, Insulation and Nutrients

1) Fats are used by the body for energy.

2) Fats form an insulating layer under your skin to keep you warm.

3) They're also used to protect your bones, arteries and organs, such as your kidneys.

4) They're a source of fat-soluble vitamins (e.g. A and D — p.57) and help the body absorb these vitamins.

5) There are two main types of fat — unsaturated and saturated.

Unsaturated fats

- Unsaturated fats are usually healthier than saturated fats. These can be monounsaturated fats and polyunsaturated fats.
- Foods such as seeds, oily fish and vegetable oils are high in unsaturated fats.

Saturated fats

- Saturated fats are usually classed as unhealthy fats, especially if eaten in large amounts.
- Foods such as meat, butter and cheese are high in saturated fats.

- Omega-3 and omega-6 are essential fatty acids, which are types of polyunsaturated 'healthy fats'.
- Our body can't produce these, so we have to consume them as part of our diet.
- Omega-3s are found in foods such as oily fish and seeds.
- Omega-6s are found in foods such as chicken, nuts and vegetable oils.

Some people take fish-oil capsules to get their dose of omega-3 fatty acids.

6) Foods are often fried and roasted in fats. The food absorbs the fat used, which increases the fat and energy content of the dish. However, cooking in fat for a short period, such as stir-frying, can help with the absorption of other important nutrients, e.g. vitamin A (see p.57).

7) Some fats can be damaged at high temperatures, though. E.g. fish containing omega-3 fatty acids can be better preserved by boiling compared to frying or microwaving.

8) Some fats, e.g. oils, can cause toxic substances to form when heated at a high temperature for too long.

Save money on heating by regularly eating an entire wheel of brie...

Fats have a bad reputation, but as you can see, they are essential for a healthy diet. The key thing is making sure you're eating the right types of fats, and ensuring you're cooking them in a suitable way.

Proteins and Carbohydrates

Now onto proteins and carbohydrates — two more types of macro-nutrient essential for good health...

Protein is Needed for Growth, Repair and Maintenance

1) Our bodies need protein for growth, cell repair and maintenance, and as a secondary source of energy.
2) Protein is made up of building blocks called amino acids.
3) Some amino acids are essential for our bodies — these are ones our bodies can't make themselves.
4) Proteins have different biological values based on the amino acid content:

High biological value (HBV) proteins

- HBV proteins contain all of the essential amino acids we need.
- They're mainly found in animal sources — e.g. meat, fish, poultry, eggs, cheese and milk. They're also found in some plant-based sources — e.g. soya beans and quinoa.

Low biological value (LBV) proteins

- LBV proteins are missing one or more of the essential amino acids we need.
- They're only found in plant sources — e.g. peas, lentils, nuts, seeds and most beans, and in smaller amounts in vegetables like spinach and broccoli.

5) When protein is cooked (e.g. by frying or baking) or exposed to acid (e.g. lemon juice), it starts to break down. This changes the texture of the food and makes it more digestible.
6) However, protein is destroyed when it is overcooked. Cooking methods such as boiling, grilling and roasting, where a high temperature is used, make overcooking much more likely. Protein is less likely to be overcooked when steamed.

Carbohydrates are Needed for Energy

1) Carbohydrates mainly provide the body with energy.
2) There are two main types of carbohydrate — simple and complex:

- Simple carbohydrates (e.g. sugar) are sugars made up of one or two sugar molecules (e.g. glucose and sucrose). They are digested rapidly, so eating them can cause blood sugar levels to go up very quickly. This provides a short burst of energy.
- They're found in 'sugary' foods such as cakes, jams, sweets and fizzy drinks, but are also found in fruits, vegetables and dairy products.

- Complex carbohydrates (e.g. starch) are made up of lots of sugar molecules. They take longer to digest, so provide energy for longer.
- They're found in foods such as bread, pasta, potatoes, rice and cereals.

3) When starch is cooked in liquid, such as during boiling, it becomes gelatinised (turns to a jelly-like consistency). This makes it much easier to digest. Gelatinisation also happens during cooking methods such as baking or stir-frying when the starch absorbs water or oil that's present.
4) Sugars dissolve in water, so blanching (see p.76) or boiling fruits and vegetables, or canning them, can result in a loss of sugars.

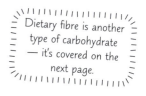

Dietary fibre is another type of carbohydrate — it's covered on the next page.

That youth's no amateur... he's a pro-teen...

That's it for macro-nutrients that provide us with energy. As the name suggests, they're a large part of our nutrition and you need to know the role each of them plays in our diet. Now, anyone for a slice of cake?

Unit 2: Section 1 — The Importance of Nutrition

Fibre, Water and Minerals

We also need fibre, water and small amounts of minerals in our diet — this nutrition lark is full of surprises...

Dietary Fibre Isn't Digested by the Body

1) Dietary fibre, sometimes called NSP (non-starch polysaccharide), is a type of carbohydrate (see previous page) that helps to keep your digestive system working properly and keeps food moving through it.

2) There are two main components of dietary fibre:

   - Soluble fibre — dissolves in water to form a gel, which helps with digestion.
   - Insoluble fibre — brings water into your stool (poo) to make it softer and easier to pass.

3) Fibre is found in foods like fruits, vegetables, wholegrain foods (e.g. wholemeal bread), beans and pulses.

You Can't Live Without Water

- Around 60% of your body is water — it's found in every cell of your body, as well as fluids like blood, sweat and saliva.
- Our bodies need water to eliminate waste from the body, control body temperature (e.g. by sweating) and aid the process of digestion.
- You get water from drinks like water (obviously), fruit juice, tea, lemonade, etc. It's also found in food — vegetables and fruit contain quite a lot, and even things like meat and bread contain water.

Our body loses water in lots of ways, e.g. sweat, breath, urine and faeces. If you don't drink enough to replace the water you've used or lost, you become dehydrated.

Calcium, Iron, Magnesium, Sodium and Potassium are Minerals

Minerals are chemical elements that our bodies need in small amounts. They help in various chemical reactions in our body and are needed for a variety of reasons:

Mineral	What it's needed for	Sources include
Calcium	Strong bones and teeth, healthy nerves and muscles and helps make sure blood clots normally.	Milk, cheese, tofu, bread, hard water, green leafy vegetables, sesame seeds.
Iron	Forms part of haemoglobin which gives blood cells their red colour and carries oxygen to body cells.	Dark green vegetables (e.g. spinach) and meat (especially liver and kidney).
Magnesium	Healthy bones and helps release energy from our food.	Green leafy vegetables (e.g. spinach), nuts, seeds, dark chocolate.
Sodium (from salt)	Helps control blood pressure, muscle contraction and nerve function. It also helps cells take up water and nutrients.	Savoury sauces, processed meats, canned fish, cheese.
Potassium	Good cardiovascular health and for controlling the balance of fluids in our body — it even works with sodium to control our muscles and nerves.	Fruit and veg (especially bananas), pulses, nuts and seeds.

Fibre Optics — a range of light snacks to aid digestion...

Don't get confused — while fibre isn't digested by the body, it plays a very important role in our digestive system. If you don't eat enough fibre, it can lead to health problems such as constipation and bowel cancer.

Unit 2: Section 1 — The Importance of Nutrition

Vitamins

As well as fats, proteins, carbohydrates, fibre, water and minerals, we also need vitamins — blimey!

Vitamins A and D are Fat-Soluble

1) Fat-soluble vitamins are found in fatty foods (e.g. meat, fish, animal-based products and vegetable oils).

2) There are two fat-soluble vitamins you need to know about — meet vitamins A and D:

Vitamin	What it's needed for	Sources include
A	Good vision (especially when it's dark), growth, healthy skin and immune system.	Fish, eggs, butter, oranges, dark green vegetables.
D	Along with calcium, it helps your body make strong bones and teeth.	Egg yolks and oily fish.

The amount of vitamin A that can be absorbed from some vegetables can be increased by using fat from frying (see p.54).

B Vitamins and Vitamin C are Water-Soluble

1) 'Water-soluble' vitamins dissolve in water.

Vitamin	What it's needed for	Sources include
B_1	Helps the nervous system and with energy release from foods.	Bread, pasta, rice, peas, eggs and liver.
B_2	Helps with energy release from foods and repair of tissues.	Milk, eggs, cheese, and leafy greens.
B_3	Helps with energy release from foods and maintaining a healthy nervous system and skin.	Wheat, nuts, meat and fish.
B_9	Crucial for growth, healthy babies and works with vitamin B_{12} to make red blood cells.	Liver, peas and leafy greens.
B_{12}	Helps the nervous system and works with vitamin B_9 to make red blood cells.	Milk, eggs, meat and fish.
C	Protects the body from infection and allergies, keeps blood vessels healthy and heals wounds. It also helps the body absorb iron.	Citrus fruits, tomatoes, strawberries, green veg and potatoes.

2) Foods need to be prepared and cooked carefully in order to keep the vitamins.

- Prepare fruits and veg just before they're needed — they start losing vitamin C once exposed to air.
- Since B vitamins and vitamin C dissolve in water, fruits and veg shouldn't be left to stand in water. Unless this liquid is also consumed, the vitamins will be lost.
- This means steaming and microwaving are preferred cooking methods to boiling and poaching, as they keep water-soluble vitamins in the food.
- The B vitamins and vitamin C can also be damaged by high heat — grilling, roasting, frying and baking can all lead to loss of vitamins.
- Stir-frying can be preferable since it doesn't involve water and the cooking time is short, so there's less loss of vitamins compared to some other methods.

Chopping fruit and veg into small pieces exposes more of the surface to air and water, so vitamins are more likely to be lost.

Vitamin B Group? — my dad's got one of their records...

Fat-soluble vitamins that aren't used by the body are stored in our fat tissue for future use. Water-soluble vitamins aren't generally stored in the body though, so we need to make sure we consume them daily.

Unit 2: Section 1 — The Importance of Nutrition

A Balanced Diet

To get all the nutrients you need, it's recommended your diet contains certain amounts of different food groups.

There are Five Main Food Groups for a Healthy Diet

Having too much or too little of some nutrients can lead to health problems. The diagram below shows some general advice on how much or little of each food group is usually recommended.

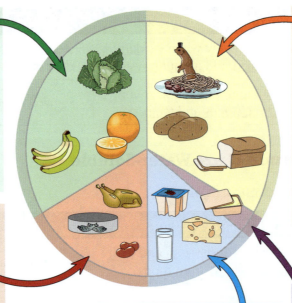

FRUIT AND VEGETABLES
- About 1/3 of your daily food intake.
- At least 5 portions of fruit and veg every day.
- One portion is, e.g. an apple, a heaped tablespoon of raisins, or 150 ml of juice.

CARBOHYDRATES
- About 1/3 of your daily food intake* should be complex carbohydrates.
- Choose higher fibre, wholegrain options with less fat, sugar and salt.
- Include a starchy food in every meal. E.g. potatoes, wholegrain bread and pasta.

*Careful here — we're talking about the amount of carbs you eat, not how much energy you get from them (see p.61).

PROTEIN
- Include two portions of fish a week (one oily, e.g. salmon, sardines).
- Pulses are a good alternative to meat.
- Choose lean cuts of meat and eat less processed meat (e.g. bacon, sausages).

DAIRY PRODUCTS AND ALTERNATIVES
- Have some dairy and try lower fat options, e.g. reduced-fat cheese.
- You can also try dairy alternatives, such as soya or rice-based drinks.

FATS
Use unsaturated oils and spreads, and not very often. E.g. sunflower and olive oil.

- Limit sugary, salty and fatty foods, e.g. muffins, cakes, biscuits.
- Drink 6-8 glasses of fluids a day — hydration is part of a healthy diet.

Although lower fat options are generally recommended, you still need to make sure you are consuming enough fats for a healthy diet, as well as the vitamins that can be lacking in 'reduced-fat' foods.

Different People Need Different Amounts of Nutrients

Dietary reference values (DRVs) are estimates of the amount of nutrients people should have in their diet. The amount of nutrients needed depends on many factors like age, sex, how active they are, and if they have any diet-related health conditions. There's more coming up on these over the next few pages.

> **EXAMPLE**
>
> 1) An average male should eat 55 g and an average female should eat 45 g of protein each day.
> 2) In reality, the amount of protein different people need varies:
>
> - Growing children need a greater amount of protein relative to their size and body mass.
> - Physically active people need more protein for muscle growth and repair.
> - Pregnant women need about 6 g more protein than normal to help the baby grow. During breastfeeding, women require even more.

If only custard creams were 1 of your 5 a day...

Food packaging often shows the dietary reference values for different nutrients. It's important to remember that these are just an average amount, and that realistically the amounts needed depend on the individual.

Unit 2: Section 1 — The Importance of Nutrition

Nutrition at Different Life-Stages

This page will give you the low-down on how nutritional needs change as we get older.

Children Grow Quickly and Need Lots of Energy

Babies (0-1 year)
1) Babies grow and develop rapidly, so it's important they're getting all the nutrients, especially protein, vitamins and minerals. Babies get more active as they get older, and so need more food for energy.
2) Babies get all of their nutrients from breast milk or baby formula milk, until they start being weaned at around 6 months old, where other foods are slowly introduced.
3) Salt and simple sugars should be kept at a minimum.

Before 6 months, babies get water from breast milk or baby formula. Then up until they're 4, the amount needed gradually increases from sips with meals to 5 glasses/day. Children aged 4-13 should have 5-8 glasses/day, and teenagers should have 6-8 glasses/day.

Toddlers (1-3 years)
1) Toddlers (and children up until the age of five) should gradually move towards the recommended diet shown on the previous page so that they get all of the nutrients they need as they grow and develop.
2) Toddlers do not have large stomachs, so should have small, frequent meals to get the energy they need.
3) 350 ml of milk per day gives them the daily calcium they need and is a good source of vitamin A.

It's actually better to get calcium from a range of foods, rather than just from milk.

Babies, toddlers and younger children should have full-fat dairy products instead of reduced-fat options as they are still growing and so still require all of the nutrients.

Children (4-12 years)

Nutrient	What it's needed for	Example foods
Protein	To help them grow and repair the body.	fish fingers, boiled eggs
Carbohydrate	Starchy carbohydrates and some fats provide energy for growth and physical activity. They need more than adults (in proportion to their body size). Saturated fats should be eaten in moderation.	mashed potato, pasta
Fat		peanuts, avocados
Calcium	For healthy teeth and bone development.	milk, yoghurt tubes, cheese
Vitamin D		tuna, salmon

Foods high in sugar should be eaten infrequently, and only ever at mealtimes. Too many of these foods can cause tooth decay and weight gain unrelated to normal growth.

Teenagers (13-19 years)

Nutrient	What it's needed for	Example foods
Protein	To cope with rapid growth spurts. Boys tend to need more protein than girls as muscular tissue develops.	omelettes, chicken
Iron	Teenage girls who have periods lose iron, which needs to be replaced or they could become iron deficient (see p.62). Vitamin C helps the body absorb the iron.	spinach, beef
Vitamin C		peppers, strawberries
Calcium	The skeleton grows quickly during this time. These nutrients are necessary as they help the skeleton reach peak size and bone density.	milk, yoghurt, kale, tofu
Vitamin D		tuna, salmon, mackerel

During the teen years there can be lots of stress (e.g. exams, media pressure), which affects eating habits — stress can lead to conditions like anorexia, or overeating which can cause obesity.

A quick way to balance your diet? Eat standing on one foot...

In the controlled assessment, you may have to plan a dish for somebody of a certain age, so make sure you know how the nutritional needs of young people and adults (see next page) change as they get older.

Unit 2: Section 1 — The Importance of Nutrition

Nutrition at Different Life-Stages

Adults Stop Growing and Nutritional Needs Don't Vary Much

Early / Middle Adulthood

1) Growth and development stops, so adults should focus on maintaining a healthy lifestyle — they are encouraged to follow a balanced diet (see p.58) to keep the body disease-free.

2) Men usually require more calories than women because they have more lean muscle (muscles require lots of energy to function properly) and are generally taller and larger.

3) Basal metabolic rate (see next page) slows down as adults reach middle age, so it's important to balance energy intake with energy burned to prevent excessive weight gain.

4) Iron is especially important for adult women who lose it through periods.

5) Calcium and vitamin D are important for all adults to reduce the chance of developing bone diseases in later life — women can quickly lose bone strength after the menopause in their 40s or 50s too, so these nutrients are needed to keep the skeleton strong.

This counts as a balanced diet, right?

Adults should aim to drink 6-8 glasses of water per day to keep hydrated.

Late Adulthood

1) As we age, our muscle mass decreases and it can become more difficult to do physical exercise — elderly adults can gain body fat if their diet doesn't change.

2) Elderly adults need to take great care with their energy intake — cutting down on excess saturated fats will help avoid health risks like cardiovascular disease (see page 62).

3) The senses of taste and smell change, which can affect the enjoyment of food and decrease appetite. Recipes and meals need to be adapted to make them appealing and interesting.

4) Elderly adults have similar nutritional requirements to younger adults, but they must make sure they get enough:

Nutrient	Reason	Example Foods
Calcium	To help stop bones becoming weak and brittle and reduce the risk of developing bone diseases.	milk, yoghurt, kale, sardines
Vitamin D		tuna, salmon, mackerel
Vitamin B$_{12}$	To keep the brain healthy and prevent memory loss.	milk, fish, beef
Fibre	To help prevent constipation as the digestive system begins to weaken.	lentils, wholemeal bread
Vitamin A	To help maintain good eyesight.	liver, scrambled eggs

5) Vitamin supplements are useful if your diet doesn't contain enough, e.g. less active elderly adults may not get enough vitamin D from sunlight, so may benefit from vitamin D tablets.

Oh, I thought *supple*ments helped you be more flexible...

In adults, it's less about providing energy and nutrients for growth and development, and more about keeping healthy and free from diet-related health issues (see p.62 for more on some of these).

Unit 2: Section 1 — The Importance of Nutrition

Special Dietary Needs — Lifestyle

BMR and PAL are key terms to do with energy and diet. Are you ready? Let's go...

BMR is the Minimum Energy Needed to Function

1) Basal Metabolic Rate (BMR) is the smallest amount of energy needed for you to stay alive — this is stuff you don't think about, like breathing and keeping your heart beating.

2) These basic life processes can use up to about 75% of the energy we use each day — other things like digestion and physical activity make up the rest.

3) There are many factors that affect a person's BMR:

4) The higher your BMR, the more calories you need. Calories are just a measure of energy, e.g. in food.

- Age — BMR decreases as we get older due to reduction of muscle mass.
- Sex — females, in general, have a lower BMR than males as they're generally smaller and tend to have less muscle.
- Weight and height — heavier or larger bodies need more calories, so have a higher BMR.
- Exercise — again, it's all about muscle. Regular exercise (especially strength training) increases muscle, which raises your BMR.

The average BMR for an adult is about 1500 – 2000 kcal.

PAL is a Way to Express Your Physical Activity

1) Your Physical Activity Level (PAL) is a measure of how active you are or how much exercise you get. Someone who's active will have a higher PAL than someone with a sedentary (inactive) lifestyle.

2) Peoples' jobs can have a big effect on their PAL, as it's what they spend a lot of their time doing — a competitive gymnast is likely to have a higher PAL than someone who sits at a desk all day.

3) BMR and PAL multiplied together give your daily energy requirement:

CGP editor (with little daily exercise) PAL = about 1.6

Daily energy requirement (kcal) = BMR × PAL

Competitive gymnast PAL = about 2.2

4) You have to balance your energy intake to maintain a healthy weight:
- If you consume more energy than you use you will gain weight.
- If you consume less energy than you use you will start to lose weight.

5) This energy balance can change throughout life — for example:
- As you get older your BMR decreases, so you'll need fewer calories to maintain a healthy weight.
- Generally, older people also have less active lifestyles than children and middle-aged adults, causing a decrease in PAL. This also means fewer calories are needed to maintain a healthy weight.

Have the Right Balance of Energy Sources

Carbohydrates, fats and proteins are our main sources of energy.

The recommended proportion of energy from different macro-nutrients per day is:

Try to get a good variety, if eating low biological value proteins (see p.55).

Carbohydrates 50%
Protein 15%
Fat 35%

- The majority should come as starches and as sugars present in milk and fruit.
- No more than 5% should come from sugar added to processed foods.

- Getting less than 35% is fine.
- Try to eat less saturated fat.

As well as increasing the amount of energy-giving foods we need to eat, physical activity also increases the amount of water lost in sweat and breath — you need to drink more water to replace it and stop dehydration.

How to increase your PALs — go to lots of parties...

Remember, each person will need different amounts of energy depending on their BMR and their PAL. So the amount of energy you need to maintain a healthy weight probably won't be the same as your best mate.

Unit 2: Section 1 — The Importance of Nutrition

Special Dietary Needs — Medical Conditions

You may have to plan a meal for someone with a dietary need — diet-related health problems, pregnancy, intolerances, allergies, and ethical and religious beliefs all affect what people eat.

Medical Conditions can have Different Dietary Needs

Cardiovascular disease (CVD) refers to any disease related to the heart or blood vessels.

TYPE 2 DIABETES

People with Type 2 diabetes need to control their blood sugar levels.

1) Avoid added sugar or use natural sweeteners, such as stevia.
2) Use foods that are digested slowly (such as brown rice or quinoa) so that blood sugar levels are raised gradually.

CARDIOVASCULAR DISEASE (CVD)

People with CVD need to lower their calorie intake and reduce the amount of salt, sugar and saturated fat.

1) Use correct portion sizes to control the amount of calories in a meal.
2) Reduce saturated fat by using vegetable oils for frying and use cooking methods that don't add extra fat (e.g. grilling).
3) Replace fatty and sugary foods with more fruit and veg.
4) Salt intake should be reduced to help lower blood pressure.

PREGNANCY

Pregnant women should adapt their diet to help the baby.

1) Women need about 200 more calories per day towards the end of the pregnancy to support the baby's growth. However, overeating can cause excessive weight gain.
2) They should consume more vitamin B_9 (see p.57), e.g. from leafy greens, to help reduce the risk of birth defects.
3) Avoid certain food and drink such as liver products, unpasteurised dairy, pâté and alcohol. Limit others, such as tuna and caffeine.

IRON DEFICIENCY

People with iron deficiency need good sources of iron in their diet (and vitamin C to help the body absorb it).

1) Include foods high in iron, e.g. red meat, dark-green leafy vegetables and iron-fortified cereals.
2) Include foods high in vitamin C, e.g. tomatoes and citrus fruits.

Warning: iron deficiency.

People with Intolerances and Allergies Can't Eat Certain Foods

Individuals with allergies and intolerances (see p.46-47) need to avoid eating foods containing the allergen or substance they are intolerant to. They can often substitute foods for something similar.

Condition	Things to avoid	Substitutions
Lactose intolerance	Lactose — a sugar found in milk and milk-based ingredients.	• Lactose-free drinks, such as soya or almond drink. • Dairy products, e.g. cheese and yoghurt, have lactose-free alternatives.
Gluten intolerance	Gluten found in wheat, barley and rye and products made with them.	• Alternative flours, e.g. coconut, tapioca or rice flours are all gluten-free alternatives to wheat flour.
Allergies	Any products containing the allergen or traces of the allergen, e.g. nuts, milk, eggs and seafood.	• Will depend on the allergen. • E.g. nuts aren't vital for a balanced diet, so substitutions can be made. Some biscuit and cake recipes only use nuts to add flavour, so the nuts can just be removed.

My cardiovascular system never loved me — such heartache...

If you need to plan a dish for somebody with an allergy or intolerance, bear in mind that alternative ingredients (e.g. gluten-free bread) are often more expensive, and so this can increase the cost of the dish.

Unit 2: Section 1 — The Importance of Nutrition

Special Dietary Needs — Personal Beliefs

Many cultures and religions have their own customs around what they do and don't eat.

Personal Choices can be Based on Moral or Ethical Concerns

1) Personal choice is often based on a person's idea of what is right and wrong (their 'moral' and 'ethical' concerns).

2) Animal welfare is a concern for many. People may choose to eat foods where they know the animals have been treated ethically, e.g. free-range products, or they may avoid meat altogether.

- A vegetarian is someone who chooses not to eat any meat (and sometimes products derived from animals, like milk and eggs) due to personal or religious beliefs.
- Vegans do not eat any meat, fish or animal products.
- Pescatarians do not eat meat, but do consume fish and animal products, e.g. eggs, cheese and milk.

3) Dishes with vegetables are generally healthy and nutritionally balanced, but you will have to include protein from alternative sources to meat (see p.55), such as tofu and Quorn™.

Be careful of hidden animal-based ingredients, such as gelatine (used in jelly and marshmallows) and rennet (used in some cheeses).

Different Religions have Different Views on Food

Many religions have specific dietary laws and rules that should be followed:

Judaism

1) Jewish dietary laws (kashrut) state that their food must be kosher (meaning fit for consumption).
2) Kosher animals are ones that have split hooves and chew cud (such as cows and deer), plus fish that have fins and scales (so no shellfish). These must be prepared according to kashrut.
3) Jews are not allowed to eat pig, rabbit, hare, camel and many other animals.
4) Dairy and meats must not be cooked together or eaten together as a mixture.

Islam

1) The Qur'an states that meats eaten by Muslims must be halal — where the lawful animal is slaughtered in a specific way whilst being blessed.
2) Muslims cannot eat pork, nor any product made from pigs, such as gelatine.
3) Muslims are not allowed to drink alcohol.
4) During the period of Ramadan, Muslims fast between sunrise and sunset.

Sikhism

1) Baptised Sikhs are prohibited from eating meat which is ritually slaughtered (such as halal or kosher meat). They also can't drink alcohol.
2) Many Sikhs are vegetarian.

Hinduism

1) Many Hindus are vegetarian, but some avoid certain vegetables that are considered harmful, e.g. garlic, onion and mushrooms.
2) Cows are sacred in Hinduism, so most Hindus will avoid eating any beef.
3) Hindus are not allowed to drink alcohol.
4) Only pure foods (like fruit or yoghurt) can be eaten during periods of fasting.

Buddhism

Buddhists believe that all living beings are sacred, so the majority of Buddhists are vegetarian or vegan (although there are no strict rules on this).

Rastafarianism

1) Eating pork is forbidden in Rastafarianism.
2) Many Rastafarians stick to an I-tal (clean and natural) diet that's mainly made up of fresh vegetables.

In a pickle? Time to wrap your head around these dietary (s)laws...

It's important to respect the views of individuals when it comes to planning a dish for them. You should always be mindful of their personal choices, whether these are based on religious laws or ethical reasons.

Unit 2: Section 1 — The Importance of Nutrition

Revision Summary for Unit 2: Section 1

That's it for all things nutrition. Now let's balance up that reading with some questions to see how much you took in.
- Tackle the summary questions below. Yes, they're hard — try to answer them from memory to really test how well you know the topic. The answers are all in the section, so go over anything you're unsure of again.
- When you've done all the questions for a topic and are completely happy with it, tick off the topic.

Nutrients, Fats, Proteins and Carbohydrates (p.54-55) ☐

1) Describe the difference between macro-nutrients and micro-nutrients, giving examples of each.
2) Give three reasons why human bodies need fats.
3) Fats can be saturated or unsaturated. Give two examples of food sources that are high in each type.
4) How does using different cooking methods affect the nutritional content of a food containing fats?
5) Give three reasons why human bodies need proteins.
6) What is the difference between high biological value proteins and low biological value proteins? Give three sources of each.
7) Describe two ways to make protein more digestible.
8) Name the two main types of carbohydrate.
   For each type, describe their role in the body and give three examples of foods they're found in.
9) Give two ways that cooking carbohydrate foods can affect the nutritional value of the food.

Fibre, Water, Minerals and Vitamins (p.56-57) ☐

10) Describe the role of dietary fibre in the body and give three examples of food it can be found in.
11) Why do we need water? Give two foods and two drinks (other than water) that are sources of water.
12) Write down five minerals and explain why the body needs each one.
    Give two examples of food sources for each mineral.
13) Write down two fat-soluble vitamins and six water-soluble vitamins. For each vitamin you write down, explain why the body needs it and give an example food source.
14) Describe how to prepare and cook foods high in water-soluble vitamins in order to retain the nutritional content.

A Balanced Diet and Nutrition at Different Life-Stages (p.58-60) ☐

15) Sketch and label a pie chart showing the recommended proportions of the main food groups in a balanced diet. Give as much detail as you can about each section.
16) What are dietary reference values (DRVs)? Describe three factors that affect the DRV of protein.
17) Say as much as you can about the nutritional needs for:
    a) babies,   b) toddlers,   c) children,   d) teenagers.
18) Outline the nutritional needs for someone in early / middle adulthood.
19) Explain why it's important for elderly adults to get enough of these nutrients:
    a) calcium and vitamin D,   b) vitamin B_{12},   c) fibre,   d) vitamin A.

Special Dietary Needs (p.61-63) ☐

20) What are BMR and PAL? Explain how these values affect a person's daily energy requirement.
21) Describe two factors than can affect the number of calories needed to maintain a healthy weight.
22) What are the recommended proportions of energy from carbohydrates, fats and proteins?
23) Outline the dietary needs for a person with the following medical conditions:
    a) type 2 diabetes,   b) cardiovascular disease,   c) pregnancy,   d) iron deficiency.
24) Outline the dietary needs of somebody with:
    a) lactose intolerance,   b) gluten intolerance,   c) an allergy.
25) Describe the dietary needs of vegetarians, vegans and pescatarians.
26) Outline the dietary guidelines set out by:
    a) Judaism,   b) Islam,   c) Sikhism,   d) Hinduism,   e) Buddhism,   f) Rastafarianism.

Unit 2: Section 1 — The Importance of Nutrition

Unit 2: Section 2 — Menu Planning

Menu Planning and Costs

Catering providers need to be able to answer two key questions — what food will they offer, and how will they produce it? To know what food they're going to offer, they need to plan their menu.

Menu Planning is Essential for Successful Catering Providers

A menu is a list of all the dishes offered by a catering establishment. Menu planning just means a business deciding what food it will offer.

- For non-residential catering providers, their food is the key part of their product. There are lots of other factors that are important for a catering business, e.g. its service, location and physical environment, but producing good food is the most important.

- There are lots of things a business needs to consider when planning a menu, and having a good plan is very important to a business's success.

The next five pages cover different factors that a catering business needs to consider when planning their menu. You'll also need to consider these in the controlled assessment when discussing the factors that affected your choice of dishes. There's more about what to expect in the controlled assessment on p.84.

Businesses Need to be Profitable to Survive

1) In a non-residential catering business, the price of the food and drinks sold needs to make up for all of the business's costs (see p.17 for more on costs).

2) These costs include the cost of the ingredients used, but also all of the other things the business has to spend money on — such as wages, utility bills, rent, business rates, buying new equipment, marketing...

3) This means businesses have to get their menu pricing right — the prices need to be high enough to help the business make a profit, but still offer good value to the customer (see next page).

4) Controlling costs is also important in making a business profitable. This means making sure that the business's costs are not higher than they need to be. Ways of controlling costs include:

Residential businesses will also make money by charging guests for staying — this part of the business will also have its own costs to cover though.

- Having good portion control — businesses shouldn't serve more food than the customer really needs or wants, to avoid wasting costly ingredients. Portions should still be big enough to be satisfying and good value for money though.

- Reducing other sources of food waste. E.g. having a good stock control system (see p.30) to avoid buying too many ingredients that go off before they are needed. Businesses can also plan their menu so the same ingredient can be used in different dishes — this is called cross-utilisation of ingredients.

- Using less gas, electricity or water to produce dishes.

- Buying cheaper ingredients when this won't harm the quality of the dish. E.g. a cheaper cut of beef could be used for a slow-cooked stew but might not be suitable for a steak dish.

- Sometimes a business might have to buy more expensive ingredients. E.g. alternatives for people with dietary requirements (like products free from dairy or gluten) are often more expensive than the ingredients they replace.

5) Non-commercial catering providers (see pages 3-4) are not profit-making. However, they still need to control their costs to run within their budgets.

No, I said make the business profitable...

Businesses want to make money? Well I never...

The news about businesses wanting to make a profit might not be much of a surprise, but it's really important to keep in mind. Don't forget the last point though — there are other types of catering provider.

Customer Needs and Business Identity

We've covered what a business wants to do (make a profit), but what customers want is also very important.

Businesses Must Meet Customer Needs

Unsurprisingly, if catering businesses want to be successful, they need customers to want to buy their products. This means they have to offer something that meets the needs and wants of their intended customers.

Customer feedback helps businesses identify which needs they are meeting well and where they need to improve.

The menu should offer the right food for the occasion:
- Different types of food are usually eaten at different times of day, e.g. a light sandwich might be a popular choice at lunchtime but not in the evening.
- The time of year also affects the type of food customers might want, e.g. warm, hearty food is more popular in winter.
- There are also traditional foods for certain times of year, e.g. a bakery might add Christmas cakes to its offering in December.

Businesses might want to adapt their menus for different times of day/year, and might offer special menus for holidays.

Yum...

The menu should be tailored to the age of their intended customers. E.g. if their customers include families, the business could offer different menus for adults and children.

The menu should include options for customers with different dietary requirements (see p.68) — such as people with allergies, vegans and vegetarians, or people following a religious diet.

Customers want food that's good value for money (see p.36). So a menu should contain dishes that can be sold at a fair price for the quality of the food.

A business that addresses environmental issues when menu planning (see p.68) will be appealing to some customers.

The location of the business can affect the menu. E.g. a business located in a less well-off area might not be able to set high prices, so won't be able to use lots of expensive ingredients in their dishes.

Businesses might change the menu periodically to keep up with current trends to appeal to customers.

A Business's Identity Affects its Menu

1) Businesses create an identity for themselves through all of the things they do — e.g. type of service and service time, price, location and physical environment...

2) Having a clear identity helps customers know what to expect from the business, and it also helps the business appeal to their intended customers.

3) The menu needs to match the business's identity. For example, if a restaurant wants to offer a fine dining experience with excellent service (and high prices), its food should also be excellent. Often these restaurants will use uncommon ingredients and present the food in an innovative way, for example, by using dry ice or presenting food in different shapes and styles.

4) Other examples of the business's identity affecting the menu could be a restaurant offering a specific national or regional cuisine, or fast-food businesses offering food that has to be quick to cook and serve.

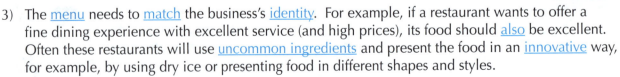

Now I know why nobody came to my barbecue in mid-January...

In the controlled assessment, you'll be given information about a business and the intended customers of your dishes, so you'll need to think about how your choice of dishes fits in with what they need.

Organoleptic Qualities

Organo-what now? Well, read on and find out — they're not as bad as they sound...

Businesses Should Consider Organoleptic Qualities

Organoleptic qualities are the properties of food that affect how we experience it through our senses.

How we sense food is key to whether we find it appetising or not. Businesses need to think about the organoleptic qualities of food when they are planning dishes. They should consider how the food affects four different senses:

Dishes need careful planning so that shapes, colours, tastes and textures are balanced.

Sight

- The presentation of a dish (how it looks) plays a big part in how appetising you find it (see p.78-79).
- Food should be neatly arranged and the plate or bowl shouldn't be too full or too empty. Having a variety of shapes and colours, and arranging food in a creative way can also make a dish look good.

Taste

- Our tongues are covered in thousands of taste buds. Each taste bud contains taste receptors that detect different chemicals in food and allow us to sense flavours.
- Flavour can be split up into five basic tastes, which are detected by the taste receptors. These are sweet, sour, salt, bitter and umami (savoury).
- Menu planners should consider whether different flavours go well together in dishes, and if any will be too overpowering. People have different preferences for taste, so a menu should also offer variety.

Touch

- The texture of food is how it feels in our mouth, e.g. firm or soft, or smooth or crunchy.
- Dishes should ideally have a mixture of textures.

Aroma

- The aroma (smell) of foods affects how we taste them. (You might have noticed that you can't taste as well if your nose is bunged up.)
- As with flavours, smells should go well together and not be too overpowering.

As well as the choice of food, other factors affect how food will be sensed. For example, using fresh food will enhance the texture, taste, aroma and appearance of a dish. The cooking method chosen can also affect all four senses, and so can cooking food incorrectly.

Customers Might Want Healthier Options

1) Menu planners need to be aware of people's need for a balanced diet (see p.58). They should take into account nutritional guidance to make sure their menu options provide people with a range of nutrients.

2) Businesses might also need to respond to demand from customers for healthier options when planning their menu. E.g. it's good to have some menu options that use healthier ingredients and cooking techniques, such as poaching instead of frying.

3) In the UK, large businesses are required to state on their menus how many calories each dish contains.

I'd like to apologise to my ears for missing them off this page...

You'll need to consider all organoleptic qualities throughout the controlled assessment — no one will want to eat an overcooked and flavourless dish, no matter how beautifully presented it is.

Unit 2: Section 2 — Menu Planning

Dietary Requirements and Sustainability

On with two important but quite different things to consider — special dietary needs and the environment.

Some Customers have Dietary Requirements

As well as general nutritional advice (see the previous page), businesses need to be aware of customers' dietary requirements when planning their menus.

You'll need to consider any nutritional and dietary needs of the customer groups in the controlled assessment.

- Some people have allergies or intolerances (p.46-47) that mean they need to avoid certain types of food. E.g. people can be allergic to nuts or eggs, or have an intolerance of gluten or lactose.
- Other medical conditions also affect people's diet, such as Type 2 diabetes (see p.62 for more).
- Menus should include options suitable for people with common allergies, intolerances and other medical conditions.
- For the safety of customers, it needs to be clear on the physical menu which dishes contain which allergens. If there's no suitable option on the main menu, staff need to know how to adapt it to the customer's needs.

When menu planning, bear in mind that you'll need time and space to prepare allergen-free dishes away from the allergen to prevent contamination.

- Some people choose to exclude certain foods from their diet. For example, vegetarians don't eat meat, while vegans don't eat any animal products at all. People's religion is also an influence on their diet. There's more on personal choices on page 63.
- Businesses should aim to plan a menu that has at least one option for everyone. E.g. the menu should have vegetarian/vegan options, and a meat option that doesn't include beef or pork (which should be suitable for most religious people who want a meat dish). Businesses with a lot of inclusive options might be able to use this to appeal to customers.
- As with allergies and intolerances, it's important to make sure the descriptions on menus clearly say what's in the dishes.

Environmental Issues are Important to People

1) Businesses should be aware of their environmental impact (see p.19-20) when planning menus, particularly if they think environmental issues are important to their intended market. These issues might be important to the employees, business owners or local people too.

2) Menu planners can make a business more sustainable (see p.19) by considering the 'three Rs':

Reduce
- Food waste can be reduced by planning ahead to only buy what is needed.
- Reducing the use of energy, water and raw materials is the place where the choice of menu has the most impact. For example, businesses can choose cooking methods that use less energy and water. E.g. steaming food uses less water than boiling it.
- Businesses can reduce their environmental impact by using more sustainable ingredients. Adapting the menu to use local, seasonal ingredients could help reduce the energy required to grow and transport the ingredients.

The sustainability of ingredients depends a lot on the supplier. A supplier may be local and offer seasonal produce, but could still be run in an environmentally damaging way.

Reuse
Reusing surplus food is one way to reduce waste. E.g. leftover bones from a roast can be used with extra vegetables to make stock.

Recycle
Businesses can opt for ingredients that have recyclable or compostable packaging. They should also have places to separate waste that's recyclable and compostable from the bits that aren't.

My favourite ice cream's the 'three Rs' — rum, raisin and more rum...

The little things a business can do to be more sustainable all boil down to reducing the amount of stuff used (e.g. buying less or using less energy), or the amount of stuff wasted (e.g. by finding other uses for waste).

Practical Requirements for Menu Planning

Don't forget that a menu needs to be practical — you've got to be able to actually make the food.

The Business Must be Able to Actually Deliver its Menu

1) Over the last four pages, you've seen why businesses need to plan their menus to meet a variety of customer needs. It's also absolutely crucial for businesses to plan menus that they can actually make — they must take into account what resources they have, including their equipment, staff and time.

2) Businesses also need to be adaptable — they have to be able to do things a bit differently from the plan when needed. E.g. the availability of ingredients should be considered when menu planning, but if there's a temporary shortage of an ingredient, the business will need to adapt to do without it.

Some Dishes Require Special Equipment

- The equipment a business has affects what it can offer on its menu. Larger businesses may have more money and space for better or more specialised equipment.
- Equipment can vary from large, specialist electrical appliances to small hand-held utensils.
- The identity of the business could depend on having certain specialist equipment — e.g. a coffee shop with a commercial coffee machine, or a pizzeria with a traditional pizza oven.

See p.27-28 for more on types of catering equipment.

Chefs' Skills Affect What They Can Cook

1) Some dishes require complex skills to make, and some chefs are more experienced and skilful than others. Businesses need to account for the skill level of people in the kitchen when planning their menu (and make sure new staff have the right skills).

2) Menu planners need to consider all the different skills needed to produce dishes, including preparation, cooking and presentation skills. They should also consider what level of skill is needed to match the identity of the business and its customer needs. E.g. a big, fancy hotel with fine dining might need multiple experienced chefs with different specialised skills.

3) Chefs with a higher skill level should also be able to work more efficiently — so would be able to do more in the same amount of time.

There's more about skills on p.74-79.

Different Businesses Have Different Amounts of Time and Space

- Customers' expectations of the time taken to be served depend on the business. Customers may wait longer in a restaurant than for fast food, but still expect to be served in a reasonable amount of time.
- Having menu options where much of the work can be done in advance helps businesses prepare dishes quickly after receiving an order — some businesses buy food that's already partly prepared, or prepare food at a different location. Businesses can also plan their menus so different dishes can be prepared at the same time, by using dovetailing (see next page).
- Businesses catering for very large numbers of people might not offer as much choice or ask for choices in advance (e.g. catering for a big wedding reception).
- The amount of space available also depends on the type of business, and affects whether the menu can be delivered. Larger businesses have more space for storage, as well as for preparing multiple dishes at once, so can make a wider variety of dishes in the same amount of time.

There should be an absolutely hilarious joke here, but I ran out of sp...

There was a lot to take in on those five pages. The key thing to remember is that a menu must be desirable to customers (it has to meet their needs), as well as being achievable and profitable for the business.

Unit 2: Section 2 — Menu Planning

Planning Production

This next bit is all about how to plan dishes for a menu — there's lots to consider, from the ingredients you need, to the order of cooking. And you need to have a back-up plan in case something goes wrong...

First You Need to Decide What You're Going to Cook

1) Planning production is vital for catering providers as they'll have a limited time to prepare their dishes. You'll also need to consider this when preparing dishes, such as the ones in the controlled assessment.

2) You need to know how many dishes you're going to create and what courses they are, as well as any accompaniments. In the controlled assessment, you'll need to choose dishes that meet the brief.

3) Once you know what you're going to make, you need to work out everything you're going to need:

Ingredients	Equipment	Storage
List all the ingredients you'll need — don't forget garnishes and decorations. Include the amounts of each ingredient, e.g. in grams, millilitres etc. This is called a commodity list.	Once you know how you'll prepare, cook and present your dishes, make a list of all the equipment you'll need (see p.27-28). Work out if you'll need any specialist equipment before starting, e.g. a deep-fat fryer.	Note where ingredients should be stored and at what temperatures (see p.50). Think about how ingredients and equipment can be stored tidily, so they're easy to access but there is space to work.

Work Out Your Timings Before You Start

1) You might have a time limit in which you need to prepare and serve your dishes — keep this in mind when deciding what to cook. It'll help make sure your plan is realistic and achievable.

2) There will be lots of steps in your plan, and you'll need to prepare multiple elements, before bringing them together at the end. Some elements will take longer to create than others, so it can all get a bit complicated.

3) Working out the order you're going to do everything in before you start will make the process a lot easier.

4) First, list all the steps needed to create each dish. Then write down how long you expect each step to take. Remember to include time for plating-up and garnishing, and leave enough time for things to cook and set.

5) When you're cooking more than one dish at once, dovetailing can help you make the most of your time:

- Dovetailing (or sequencing) is where you make more than one dish at a time by switching between tasks on each recipe to help ensure you use your time efficiently.
- You should start with elements that take the longest time, e.g. you'd need to bake a cake early on to allow time for it to cook, cool and be decorated.
- Dovetailing works well when one of the tasks doesn't require your full attention, e.g. you can focus on another task whilst you've got a cake baking in the oven.
- If you've got complicated tasks that require a lot of attention, such as caramelising sugar, it's best to do them one at a time. If you try to do too much at once, something is more likely to go wrong.

6) Once you've worked out the best ways to use dovetailing in your plan, write down the order in which you're going to complete all your tasks. Making a plan like this can take a long time, but it helps make sure each dish is prepared to a high standard, at the right time, and that nothing is missed.

7) You should include quality points in your plan to show how you'll ensure your dish is of a good quality. For example, by not over-mixing things or checking a cake is cooked by sticking a skewer through it.

Plan: Put bread in toaster, toast, put toast on plate, serve...

Remember, some elements can be made well in advance of when they're needed. So, you could make a sauce early and reheat it just before it's going to be served. This is another example of using dovetailing.

Planning Production

Mise en Place Makes Cooking Run Smoother

1) 'Mise en place' means setting up everything you need before you begin cooking.
2) First, read through the recipe to work out what could be done in advance.
3) There are lots of things you can do at the start to help the rest of your time in the kitchen run smoothly. You should include these in your plan:

- Gather any equipment you'll need and make sure it's clean.
- Set up your workspace so it's tidy and you can access everything you'll need.
- Wash any fresh ingredients like fruit and veg.
- Measure out ingredients. Remember to store them correctly until they're needed.
- Prepare any ingredients and garnishes you can in advance, e.g. peel and chop carrots, or grind spices.

It might be more efficient to do some of these things later on, as part of dovetailing. It all depends on what dishes you're making.

4) Mise en place helps you move through the recipe faster and keeps things organised. It allows you to focus your attention on cooking, as you won't have to think about preparing ingredients for the next step.

You Should Plan How Your Cooking will be Safe

Health and Safety

- Before you start cooking, you need to think about possible hazards in the kitchen and what you're going to do to minimise their associated risks (see pages 42-44).
- Remember that you can reduce the risk of some hazards occurring by wearing appropriate PPE.
- Make sure you know how to safely use and operate any equipment you'll be using.
- You should make sure you have access to any cleaning equipment that might be needed to mop up any spills to prevent accidents.

Food Safety and Hygiene

- You should state in your plan how you're going to prevent contamination at all steps, e.g. by using different coloured knives and chopping boards to prepare different food groups, and by washing hands regularly. See pages 48-50 for more on preventing contamination.
- Your plan should also include how you are going to check and maintain the quality of your ingredients, e.g. by correctly storing ingredients, looking for spoilage and checking any use-by and best before dates.
- You should also make sure your plan explains how you'll ensure that any high-risk foods have been cooked, cooled, chilled and reheated safely. E.g. you should check the core temperature of cooked red meat has reached at least 75 °C, using a temperature probe.
- If you're cooking for someone with a medical dietary requirement, you may need to consider how you'll prevent cross-contamination that could cause illness:

Unit 1 Section 4 covers food safety in much more detail if you need a reminder.

For example, you may have to prepare a gluten-free bread dough before you prepare any foods containing gluten. You would also need to thoroughly clean equipment and work surfaces between use. Factors like this will affect the order of steps in your plan, so it's important you think about this before cooking.

Mr en Place has it easy — his wife is great at planning...

You've met a lot of the food safety ideas on this page already, earlier on in the book. But now you need to think about applying it all when you're in the kitchen — and to do that, it's best to add it to a plan.

Unit 2: Section 2 — Menu Planning

Planning Production

Decide What you Want the Finished Dish to Look Like

- It can be useful to make a quick sketch of what you want the dish to look like. You could include labels on your sketch for things like garnishes, plating styles, colour schemes and portion control (see p.78-79).
- Make sure you've got all the plates or serving dishes you want to use.
- Once you've decided on the presentation, you should have a rough idea of how long plating-up and decorating is going to take — make sure you take this time into account in your plan.

You Might Not Serve Your Food Straight Away

1) If you're making more than one dish for the same person, they likely won't be served at the same time. Similarly, you might be making more than one dish to be served at the same time, but one might be ready before the others.
2) You should know from your plan if anything like this is likely to happen.

HOT HOLDING
You might make something early and hot-hold it — it must be held at 63 °C or above, for no longer than 2 hours.

COOLING
Some dishes might need to be cooled before serving, or held in the fridge or freezer until it's time to serve. Make sure they are cooled within 1.5 hours to 8 °C.

3) Including details of temperatures and timings in your plan means you're less likely to make a mistake — if you accidentally hold something at the wrong temperature, you increase the risk of making someone ill.
4) You should include details of how you are going to do this, e.g. by using temperature probes, and by setting and testing the temperatures of fridges, freezers and warming trays.

Contingencies are for if Something Goes Wrong

1) There's always a chance something could go wrong — you might burn some biscuits or cut your finger.
2) But if you know what to do in these situations, it'll be easier to solve any problems that do arise.
3) That's where contingencies come in — these are just provisions put in place for something that may or may not happen. There are lots of contingencies you could set up, for example:

- Make sure you have a bit more of each ingredient than the recipe calls for — then, if any cooking doesn't go to plan, you've got enough ingredients to start again.
- Incorporate a bit of extra time in your plan incase some things take longer than expected.
- Plan a very simple back-up dish or element incase a piece of equipment breaks.
- Have a first aid kit to hand, so you can treat any minor injuries and return to cooking afterwards.

Your Plan Should be Easy to Follow

There's a lot of detail on the last few pages, so here's a summary of everything your production plan should include.

Your production plan in the controlled assessment will be marked, so it needs to be clear to others, not just you. You might find it helpful to use a different colour for each dish to keep track of steps when dovetailing.

- ingredients and quantities
- equipment and storage
- method and timings
- skills (see p.74-77)
- temperatures
- presentation
- health, safety and hygiene
- quality points
- contingencies (where relevant)

If plan A fails, don't panic — there's 25 more letters in the alphabet...
The key thing to take away from this section is to include as much detail in your plan as you can. As soon as you start cooking, the time will fly by, so it'll be much easier if you know exactly what you've got to do.

Unit 2: Section 2 — Menu Planning

Revision Summary for Unit 2: Section 2

All this talk about menus is making me hungry. It's time to see what you can remember about menu planning.
- Tackle the summary questions below. Yes, they're hard — try to answer them from memory to really test how well you know the topic. The answers are all in the section, so go over anything you're unsure of again.
- When you've done all the questions for a topic and are completely happy with it, tick off the topic.

Factors Affecting Menu Planning (p.65-69)

1) What is menu planning? Why is it important to non-residential catering businesses?
2) Explain why it is important for a catering business to get its menu pricing right.
3) Give four ways that a business can control the costs of producing the dishes on its menu.
4) How does the time of day affect what a business might offer on its menu? What about the time of year?
5) Other than adapting to the time of day and year, give three other ways that a menu can meet customer needs.
6) How do businesses create an identity for themselves? Describe how a business's identity could affect its menu.
7) What are organoleptic qualities?
8) Describe how food should ideally be presented. Why is this important?
9) How do we use our tongues to sense flavours? State the five basic tastes that make up flavour.
10) What should you consider when planning a menu to make sure the dishes taste good? What about ensuring the dishes have a pleasant aroma and textures?
11) How can a menu meet the needs of customers who want to have a balanced diet and healthier food options?
12) Give four possible reasons why a customer might have a special dietary requirement. Describe what a business can do to meet the needs of customers with dietary requirements.
13) Give an example of how a catering business can use each of the 'three Rs' to try to be more sustainable.
14) What does it mean if a menu plan is adaptable? Give an example of a time when a menu might need to be adapted.
15) Give three factors that may affect whether or not a catering business has specialist equipment.
16) Why is the skill level of kitchen staff important to consider when planning a menu?
17) Give three ways that businesses can adapt to make sure they can serve customers in an acceptable amount of time.
18) Explain why a larger business might find it easier than a small business to produce a wide variety of dishes in an acceptable amount of time.

Planning Production (p.70-72)

19) What information about ingredients, equipment and storage should you include in a production plan?
20) Why is it important to think about timings when you're planning the production of a dish?
21) What is dovetailing in cooking? Why can it be useful?
22) Describe five tasks that you could do during mise en place.
23) Briefly describe how you should consider health and safety in a production plan.
24) Briefly describe how you should consider food safety and hygiene in a production plan.
25) Outline what you should be considering when planning the presentation of a dish.
26) Explain why it is important to include details about hot-holding and cooling in a production plan.
27) What are contingencies in a production plan? Why are they important?
28) Give three examples of contingencies you could include in a production plan.
29) Make a list of the different things you should include in a production plan.

Unit 2: Section 3 — Skills and Techniques

Preparation and Knife Techniques

Some dishes are harder to prepare than others as they require more complex skills...

There are Lots of Preparation Skills to Learn

- Preparation and knife skills are needed to get the components of a dish ready to be cooked, or plated up if they don't need cooking.
- You'll need to demonstrate a range of preparation skills during the controlled assessment. Luckily, the next couple of pages summarise all the skills you might need to use...

Some components of a dish might come already prepared, e.g. chopped carrots. Using these is classed as a basic skill.

Basic Skills are the Easiest to do

Skill	Definition	Example where it's used
Beating	Using a spoon to combine and add air to mixtures.	Cake or pancake batter.
Blending	Stirring together ingredients until just combined.	A mix of herbs and spices.
Grating	Cutting hard food into short shreds using a grater.	Cheese, carrots and chocolate.
Hydrating	Adding water to an ingredient to change its texture.	Making doughs and sauces.
Juicing	Squeezing the juice out of a fruit or vegetable.	Adding lemon juice to sauces.
Marinating	Soaking in a seasoned liquid before cooking.	To add flavour and soften meat.
Mashing	Crushing a food to a smooth mush using a masher.	Potatoes and squashes.
Melting	Heating a solid ingredient until it turns to a liquid.	Butter and sugar for flapjacks.
Proving	Leaving dough to rest before baking it.	Doughs containing yeast.
Shredding	Cutting into long thin strips using a shredder or peeler.	Cheese, carrots and courgettes.
Sieving	Putting an ingredient through a sieve.	Flour for smooth cake mixes.
Tenderising	Beating a piece of meat with a mallet to soften it.	Tough cuts of meat like brisket.
Zesting	Scraping off the outer peel of a citrus fruit.	To add flavour to bakes and sauces.

Medium Skills are a Bit Harder

Skill	Definition	Example where it's used
Creaming	Beating fats and sugars to give bakes a fluffy texture.	Sponge cake and biscuit mixtures.
Dehydrating	Removing water from an ingredient by heating.	Fruits, vegetables and some meats.
Folding	Repeatedly folding a mixture over itself until the ingredients combine.	Mixing flour into a cake mixture.
Kneading	Folding a dough containing gluten to help it rise.	Bread dough.
Measuring	Ingredients can be measured out using measuring jugs, cups or measuring spoons.	Milk, vanilla extract and spices.
Mixing	Combining ingredients with a spoon or mixer.	Sauces and soups.
Puréeing	Mashing and straining food until it is smooth.	Fruits, vegetables and pulses.
Rubbing-in	Pressing fat into flour until it resembles breadcrumbs.	Scones, biscuits and rock cakes.
Rolling	Using a rolling pin to flatten a mixture.	Pastry for tarts or dough for biscuits.
Skinning	Removing the skin from an animal.	Fish and chicken.
Toasting	Lightly browning an ingredient by putting it in the oven or in a dry frying pan under a low heat.	Nuts and seeds.
Weighing	Measuring the mass of solid ingredients with scales.	Flour, sugar and butter.

I know, this book is really grate — it's the only one you'll knead...

When you decide on what dish to create for the assessment, make sure you demonstrate a range of skills. You won't get top marks if all the components of you dish are ready-made — soup from a can won't cut it.

Preparation and Knife Techniques

Complex Skills Require the Most Practice

Skill	Definition	Examples
Crimping	Pressing together pieces of pastry to create decorative edges and hold in any fillings.	The edges of pies and other filled pastries.
Laminating	Folding and rolling butter into dough lots of times to create thin layers.	Creating puff pastry with a flaky texture.
Melting with a Bain-marie	A bowl is placed on top of a pan half-filled with hot water, to gently melt ingredients.	Melting chocolate to stop it from splitting and becoming grainy.
Piping	Creating neat, decorative designs by squeezing a mixture out of a piping bag.	Decorating a cake with icing and piping mashed potatoes.
Shaping	Making lots of uniform shapes out of a dough or mixture, usually by hand.	Bread buns, biscuits, sushi and sausage rolls.
Unmoulding	Removing a dish from the mould used to shape it.	Jellies, tarts and chocolates.
Whisking (aeration)	Incorporating air into an ingredient or mixture, often using an electric or hand whisk.	Eggs and cream are whisked to give them a lighter texture.

There are Different Ways to Chop Ingredients

Chopping something into smaller pieces is a basic knife technique, but there are different chopping methods that require a bit more skill. Most of these chopping techniques are used for fruit and veg.

Medium skills

1) Batôn — cut into thick sticks.
2) Chiffonade — cutting leafy vegetables into long, thin strips or ribbons.
3) Dicing — cutting into small cubes.
4) Slicing — cutting into thin, uniform discs/slices.

Complex skills

1) Julienne — cutting into thin strips.
2) Brunoise — food is first julienned and then diced to produce very small cubes.
3) Mincing — cutting small ingredients as finely as possible, e.g. garlic and fresh herbs.

Knives can be Used in Other Ways too

MEAT AND FISH

- Filleting a piece of meat or fish separates the flesh (the bit that gets eaten) from the bone and body.
- Deboning means removing all the bones, without damaging the piece of meat or fish.
- Filleting and deboning are complex skills that require special boning and filleting knives.
- Spatchcock is a medium skill used to cut open a bird and flatten it, so the meat cooks more evenly.

FRUIT AND VEG

- Trimming and peeling are both basic skills that can be used to prepare fruits and veg before they're chopped.
- Deseeding fruits is a medium skill and segmenting them is complex — you have to be careful not to damage the flesh.
- These are all delicate tasks that require small, lightweight knives.

Dicing is hard — I tried so many times, but I just couldn't roll a 6...

Phew, that's a whole lot of skills to learn. Complex skills can be pretty tricky to master, but make sure you've got the more basic skills nailed too — they crop up in pretty much every recipe.

Cooking Techniques

Right, so you've prepared your carrots into beautiful batôns. Now what?...

Some Cooking Techniques are More Tricky than Others

- Choosing the right cooking technique is important as it will affect the flavour, texture and nutrient content of the ingredients — it can make or break a dish.
- Just like the preparation skills on p.74-75, cooking techniques can be basic, medium or complex:

BASIC: basting, boiling, cooling, chilling, freezing, dehydrating, grilling, toasting, skimming

MEDIUM: baking, blanching, braising, deglazing, frying, griddling, pickling, reduction, roasting, setting, stir-frying, sautéing, sous vide, steaming

COMPLEX: baking blind, caramelising, deep-fat frying, emulsifying, poaching, tempering

Remember, to ensure foods are always cooked at the correct temperatures for the right amount of time.

- There are more details about these cooking techniques on this page and the next:

Water is Used to Cook in Lots of Different Ways

Skill	Definition	Examples
Boiling	Cooking food in a pan of boiling liquid, usually water. It doesn't add fat but nutrients can be lost in the water. It can affect the colour of ingredients too.	Potatoes, rice, pasta and veg.
Steaming	Cooking food with steam from boiling water or stock. No fat is added and the colour and nutrients are better retained than when boiling.	Fish, rice and veg.
Blanching	Part-boiling food for a short period before putting it in cold water, to help retain colour, texture and nutrients.	To prepare veg before freezing.
Poaching	Cooking delicate foods in a pan of liquid below its boiling point.	Eggs and fruit.
Braising	Slowly cooking food in an ovenproof pot that has a lid and contains liquid (e.g. a stock). The flavour of the liquid transfers to the food.	Big or tough joints of meat.
Sous vide	Food is sealed in a bag and cooked in a water bath at a controlled temperature.	Meat and eggs.

Food can also be Cooked Using Dry Heat

Skill	Definition	Examples
Baking	Cooking food using hot air, usually in an oven.	Cakes, potatoes and pies.
Baking blind	Baking pastry in the oven without the filling. Filling can be added part-way through if it also needs cooking.	Pies and tarts.
Griddling	Cooking on a flat, heated surface, called a griddle.	Burgers, steak and veg.
Grilling	Applying a very high heat to the surface of the food. Fat can drip out of the food, making it a healthier option.	Steak, cheese and veg.
Roasting	Cooking in an oven at a higher temperature than baking. It's often done with fat, making it a less healthy option.	Meat and potatoes.
Toasting	Cooking until brown and crispy, using a grill, toaster or fire.	Bread and nuts.

Food is often basted during roasting — fat and juices from the food are poured back on top for texture and flavour.

Hey — you're really steaming through this...

When choosing a cooking method, you should think about the colour and texture you want to achieve. You'll also have to think about how much time you have and what equipment is available to you.

Cooking Techniques

Frying is Cooking Food in Hot Fat

1) Frying uses fat (e.g. oil) heated to a very high temperature to cook food quickly.
2) The food absorbs the fat as it cooks, which adds flavour but makes it less healthy.
3) The fat should be hot to stop the food absorbing too much of it and going soggy.
4) There are a few different types of frying techniques:

Sautéing
- A small amount of fat is heated in a frying pan.
- Most foods need turning so they brown on both sides.
- Foods that can be sautéd include meat, fish and eggs.

Deep-Fat Frying
- Food is completely submerged in very hot oil.
- Delicate foods can be dipped in batter before frying, for a crispy outside and soft inside.
- Fish, chips and doughnuts can be deep-fat fried.

Stir-Frying
- A tiny bit of oil is heated in a pan, making it a healthier frying technique.
- Food cooks very quickly, so should be moved all the time so it doesn't burn.
- Vegetables can be stir-fried.

You can Add Texture and Flavour to Sauces and Gravies

- DEGLAZING — adding a liquid to a pan or tray that has been used to cook meat, to remove and dissolve cooking juices and residue. The liquid is then added to a gravy or sauce for flavour.
- REDUCTION — thickening a sauce, soup or gravy by simmering it to evaporate the water. This makes the flavour more intense.
- SKIMMING — removing fat or impurities from the surface of a sauce, soup or gravy. It makes the liquid clearer, smoother and reduces its fat content.
- EMULSIFYING — combining two ingredients that do not usually mix easily, such as oil and water. An ingredient containing an 'emulsifier' is added to aid mixing. E.g. egg yolk (containing an emulsifier) is added when making hollandaise sauce to help mix and combine the melted butter and water.

Simmering means to gently bubble a liquid below its boiling point.

Making Desserts can Require Extra Skills

1) Desserts like jelly, panna cotta and cheesecake can be made using gelatine, a thickening ingredient. The dessert mixture is usually heated to dissolve the gelatine. The mixture can then be poured into its mould. It is then cooled to room temperature and chilled in a fridge or freezer, and the gelatine causes the dessert to thicken and set.
2) Chocolate is often tempered — heated slowly and then cooled to make the chocolate smooth and shiny.
3) Sugar can be caramelised by gently heating it, creating a sugary syrup with a rich, buttery flavour.

There are Techniques to Preserve Food to Make it Last Longer

- Pickling is where an ingredient, such as onions or mackerel, is stored in a jar of brine or vinegar. This changes the texture and flavour of the ingredient.
- You can dehydrate (remove moisture from) some ingredients, such as fruit.
- Foods can be preserved by freezing them too — storing them below −18 °C (see p.50).

Pete and Petra were still waiting to be used in a dish...

This sentence needs an emulsifier...

Phew, my brain is fried after all these cooking techniques. You'll have to make a list of all the preparation and cooking techniques you use in the controlled assessment, so make sure you know what they are.

Presentation Skills and Techniques

As well as a dish tasting great, it needs to look good too...

Being Creative can Help a Dish Stand Out

Food is more appealing to customers if it's presented well.

Serving Dish
- Think about the shape, size and colour of the plate you use.
- You don't have to use a traditional ceramic plate — a wooden slab or rectangular slate can make a statement and help a dish stand out.
- Some parts of the dish could be placed in a smaller bowl on the larger plate, e.g. chips could be served in a small basket.
- Clear glass bowls, e.g. for desserts, can help make sure every element of the dish is visible.

Colour
- A variety of colours makes food look attractive. For example, it's better to accompany pale chicken with carrots rather than cauliflower. The colour of the plate is important too.
- Garnishes and decoration can also be used to add colour (see the next page).

Layout
- Using a variety of shapes of food makes dishes look more interesting.
- Stacking food is a good way to add height to a dish, but you should still be able to see every element.
- It is important that the plate is not too full — roughly two-thirds of the plate should be covered in food. This stops the dish from looking messy and helps the food stand out against the colour of the plate.

Plating Styles
- Elements of a dish are usually plated in odd quantities to help the dish look more attractive. There are lots of different plating styles that can be used, for example:

Classic — three basic items of vegetables, starch and protein in a specific arrangement.

Free form — the dish is thought of as a piece of abstract art. Sauces are an important part.

Landscape — elements are kept low lying and placed in a line across the plate.

Nordic — a minimalist style where elements are shaped and positioned using clean lines.

The Plate should be Portioned Correctly

1) There needs to be enough food that the customer feels like they have been provided with a decent-sized meal and that the amount of food they get offers good value for money.

2) However, there shouldn't be so much food that customers leave most of it on the plate because they are full. Accurate portion sizes reduces the amount of food waste.

I eat with my eyes — and to be honest, I'm pretty hungry...

It's true though, if a dish looks nice, you're much more likely to want to eat it. Taste is important too though — it's no good your dish looking like a work of art if it tastes like a dog's dinner...

Presentation Skills and Techniques

Accompaniments Should Complement the Dish

1) Accompaniments are food items served with the main part of the dish. They are there to add flavour, texture and visual interest to the dish. They shouldn't overpower the dish, though.

2) Accompaniments are more substantial than garnishes (see below), so they affect the nutritional value of the meal. They often take more time and effort to prepare and cook, too.

3) Even though they are not the main focus of the dish, it is important that accompaniments are cooked well. Customers are more likely to remember the soggy fries than the perfectly cooked fish.

4) Dishes might come with carbohydrate and fruit or veg accompaniments, as well as a sauce:

Savoury accompaniments	Sweet accompaniments
• CARBOHYDRATES — e.g. rice, bread, chips, mashed potato, pasta. • VEGETABLES — e.g. roasted veg, grilled veg, veg purée, salad. • SAUCES — e.g. gravy, jus, hollandaise sauce, salsa, guacamole.	• CARBOHYDRATES — e.g. biscuits, wafers, chocolates, meringues. • FRUIT — e.g. grilled fruit, berry compote, fruit salad. • SAUCES — e.g. chocolate sauce, cream, raspberry coulis, custard.

Add Garnishes and Decorate Your Dishes

1) Garnishes are small additions to your dish and can add extra colour, texture or flavour. These can be as simple or complicated as you want, from a slice of lemon to a flower made out of a radish.

2) Some decorations are used to add flair to the dish, but don't add flavour (e.g. gold leaf) or aren't meant to be eaten (e.g. serving the dish in a crab shell).

3) Other decorative techniques can be used, such as piping icing onto a cake, or creating a decorative pattern on top of a pie.

4) Sauces and purées can be used to decorate the plate by creating shapes like dots, swirls and smears, using tools such as plating wedges and squeeze bottles.

5) Styling your food using these techniques can make your dish look more appealing.

6) There are some more examples of garnishes for sweet and savoury dishes in the boxes below. Remember that the colour and flavour of the garnish you choose should complement the dish.

Sweet garnishes		Savoury garnishes	
• spun sugar • freeze-dried raspberries • tuile biscuits	• chopped nuts • edible flowers • shaped chocolate • dehydrated fruits	• lemon slices • croutons • breadcrumbs • seeds	• parmesan crisps • fresh herbs • pea shoots or watercress

All this hard work has got me dreaming of the summer hollandaise...

It's always best to have a plan of how you want your final dish to look — even garnishes and decorations should be thought about in advance. This helps make sure that everything on the plate is there for a reason.

Food Safety Practices

In Unit 1, you learnt a lot about the importance of food safety for catering establishments. Now it's time to put these things into practice when you're in the kitchen.

You Should Practice Good Personal Hygiene and Safety

1) Anybody preparing or cooking food for themselves or others should have good personal hygiene. This helps minimise the risk of contamination (see p.45).
2) Acting safely in the kitchen also minimises the risk of accidents happening.
3) Here's a reminder of some of the key personal hygiene and safety practices to follow. Flick back to Unit: 1 Sections 3 and 4 for more details:

You'll be marked on hygiene and safety in the controlled assessment, so it's really important you demonstrate these practices.

EQUIPMENT — E.g. use oven gloves when carrying hot trays. Clean spills up as soon as you spot them. Only use equipment that you know how to use correctly and safely.

HANDS — Wash hands before and after preparing food. Wash hands after touching high-risk foods or going to the toilet.

HAIR — Tie back long hair. Cover hair by wearing a hair net, bandana or hat.

CLOTHING — Wear a clean apron or chef whites, and non-slip, closed-toe shoes. There's more about suitable clothing on p.29.

CUTS — Handle knives carefully to try to prevent cuts. Wash any cuts immediately and cover them with a blue, waterproof plaster.

Good Food Hygiene Protects People Who Eat the Food

1) Make sure you know how to correctly store, handle and cook ingredients, especially high-risk foods. There's more details on the correct temperatures to store, cook and serve foods on p.50.
2) Check use-by and best-before dates. You should also check that food still looks fresh and hasn't spoiled, e.g. milk should not smell sour and fruit should not be bruised or mouldy.
3) Extra care should be taken if you're cooking for someone with a food allergy or intolerance, e.g. check food labels for the relevant allergen, and take precautions to avoid contaminating the dish.
4) Waste should be kept separate from preparation and cooking areas and removed from the kitchen regularly.
5) Clean worktops, equipment and utensils before you begin and keep them tidy and clean during cooking.
6) Don't sit or climb on work surfaces, and store your coats, bags and personal items outside of the kitchen.

Make Sure you Know What to do if There's an Accident

You might have taken lots of steps to minimise the risk of an accident, and carried out a detailed risk assessment (see p.42). But there's always a small chance that something might go wrong. In these cases, it's important to act safely, so nobody is put at further risk:

If someone gets ill or injured:
- Use the first aid box for minor injuries. Check where it's stored.
- If needed, get help from somebody who is first-aid trained.
- Call emergency services for serious accidents.

If there's a fire:
- Use a fire extinguisher or fire blanket to help put out a fire. Make sure you know where they are and have been trained to use them.
- Use the fire exits and head to the designated assembly point — make sure you know where these are.
- Call emergency services for fires that can't be controlled.

Another way to tell if milk is spoiled — see how demanding it is...

Hygiene and safety in the kitchen are often easier said than done, especially when you're focused on making a dish look and taste great. But it's just as important, and you'll be assessed on it too. So, wash your hands...

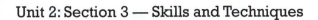

Unit 2: Section 4 — Evaluating Cooking Skills

Reviewing Dishes

When you've made a dish, you should think about what went well, and what could be improved.

You Should Evaluate Planning, Preparation and Cooking

1) For the controlled assessment, you'll be asked to plan and create two dishes — your dishes need to be suitable for the scenario and the two groups of people you are asked to cook for in the assessment.

2) Once you've created your final dishes, you'll need to write up an evaluation of how you think it all went. There are lots of areas to consider:

DISH SELECTION — Did your chosen dish contain the right nutrients for the customer, and meet any dietary requirements? Did your chosen dishes allow you to demonstrate a range of basic, medium and complex skills and techniques?

DISH PRODUCTION — Did you stick to your production plan (see p.70-72)? How did you deal with any problems?

PRESENTATION — Consider portion size, plating style, colours and garnishes (see p.78-79).

ORGANOLEPTIC QUALITIES — How was the taste, texture, aroma and appearance of the final dishes (see p.67)?

HEALTH, SAFETY & HYGIENE — Analyse how you dealt with health, safety and hygiene practices in your plan and during cooking.

WASTE — Think about how much food waste there was, and whether you followed the 3 Rs (p.20) when disposing of waste.

IMPROVEMENTS — For each of the other areas described, think about things that didn't go as well as you'd hoped. Suggest what you would do differently if you were to make the same dish again, or whether you'd change your choice of dish.

You Should Include as Much Detail as Possible

Here's a (very brief) example of how you could structure your evaluation. The more detail, explanation and description you have time to add, the better:

We've just included an evaluation for one dish here, but you'll need to evaluate both dishes you make. Remember to include coloured photographs of your dishes too

You can talk about improvements throughout the review, or put them all in a section at the end.

You need to list the skills you used.

Point out any problems you had and how you dealt with them.

Analysis: Vegan ravioli
I made a handmade ravioli with a spicy tomato sauce, finished with sprigs of parsley. The dish fit the brief for creating a main course for a vegan customer at a restaurant.

Dish Selection:
The dish was made from plant-based ingredients, so was suitable for the customer, who was vegan. It was low in saturated fat as it did not contain butter, and was also high in fibre. However, it was low in protein. This could be improved by adding a vegan protein source such as lentils. I demonstrated a range of skills:
Basic: blending, chopping, boiling
Medium: measuring, mixing, rolling, sautéing.
Complex: crimping, shaping.

Dish Production:
Overall, I managed to follow my plan well, and produced the dish on time. Some of my fresh tomatoes looked slightly bruised, so I replaced the bruised ones with some tinned tomatoes. If I were to make the dish again, I would start by making the filling rather than the pasta dough, to give it more time to cool.

Presentation:
I chose a white plate to help the colour of the dish stand out. I used a parsley garnish to decorate the dish and add colour and flavour. I was careful to plate the dish neatly, and did not overfill it.

Organoleptic qualities:
The herbs and onions I added to my tomato sauce gave a pleasant aroma. The spices were well-balanced. The texture of the pasta was a bit too soft, which could have been improved by cooking it for one minute less.

Health, Safety and Hygiene:
I wore a clean apron and tied my hair back. I kept work surfaces clean throughout cooking. I spilt some sauce on the floor but didn't clean it up straight away as I was behind on time. To protect the safety of myself and others in the kitchen, I should have cleaned it up immediately.

Waste:
I mostly used fresh ingredients so there was very little packaging waste. I washed and recycled the tins from the chopped tomatoes.

Splitting your review into sections helps ensure you cover everything.

Remember to include things you did well, as well as things you could improve on.

You'll be ravioling on the floor laughing at this...

It's important to be honest in your review — if something didn't go to plan, it's better to acknowledge it. You'll still get marks for showing you understand how an issue could be resolved if you were to do it again.

Reviewing Your Performance

You've made it to the final bit — hooray! As well as reviewing the dishes you create, you'll have to evaluate your own performance throughout the controlled assessment.

You Need to Identify Personal Strengths and Weaknesses

- There are four key skills that you need to demonstrate during the controlled assessment — decision-making, planning, organisation and time management.
- At the end of the assessment, you need to write about your performance — this is for the whole assessment, not just the practical part. You should identify your own strengths and weaknesses relating to each of these skills, and suggest improvements:

Decision-making
When making decisions during the plan, did you consider different options? Did you have any problems during the practical, or was there anything that didn't go to plan? How did you decide on the actions to take?

Planning
You should include the advantages and disadvantages of the dishes you chose — think about whether they met the needs of the customers and provision.
For written tasks, think about how you planned the structure of your writing to make sure you included everything you wanted to discuss in a logical order.

Time management
How did you manage your time during both the written tasks and the practical? Think about how you split your time up between tasks, and the order you completed tasks in. Did you use time-saving techniques like dovetailing, and start by cooking the things that would take longest?

Organisation
Did you organise your workstation in the kitchen so everything was accessible, but not in the way? Were you able to stay organised so you could stick to your plan?

Your Review Should be Specific

1) You might already know that you're good at planning or organising. But to write a top-notch review, you need to give examples of times during the assessment where you demonstrated these skills.

2) Here's an example of someone discussing their planning. Remember, a complete review would include three more sections like this, for decision-making, time management and organisation:

> **Personal Performance Review:**
> **Dishes presented:** Main — Vegetarian tofu curry with rice. Dessert — Tiramisu.
> **Planning Evaluation:**
> I planned my practical session in a logical order. For example, I used mise en place to measure all my ingredients before starting, and I used dovetailing when I whipped the cream for the dessert whilst the curry was cooking in the pan. I think my plan was good as it was easy to follow and the dishes were both made on time.
> **Advantages:** The main course I chose fit the brief of being vegetarian and high in protein, as required. The dessert would be suitable for a busy restaurant, as required by the brief, as it doesn't need cooking, so could be made early on and left to chill in the fridge.
> **Disadvantages:** The tiramisu is quite high in fat as it contains a lot of fresh cream, which may not be the best choice for adults, who should look to limit excess saturated fat intake. Using fresh cream also means the tiramisu doesn't keep fresh for long, so the restaurant could end up with a lot of waste if they don't sell all the portions in time. If I were to plan the dishes again, I would pick something lower in saturated fat, that doesn't spoil so quickly, such as sorbet.

- Strength has been identified.
- Pros and cons of the dishes chosen.
- Good level of detail and examples.
- Suggested improvements have been included.

Chocolate biscuits are a personal weakness of mine...

When you're reviewing your performance, think about what tasks you found easy and what tasks were more challenging — this can help you identify any personal strengths and weaknesses.

Unit 2: Section 4 — Evaluating Cooking Skills

Revision Summary for Unit 2: Sections 3 & 4

Time flies when you're showing off your cooking skills — now its time to test how much you really know.
- Tackle the summary questions below. Yes, they're hard — try to answer them from memory to really test how well you know the topic. The answers are all in the section, so go over anything you're unsure of again.
- When you've done all the questions for a topic and are completely happy with it, tick off the topic.

Preparation and Knife Techniques (p.74-75)

1) Briefly describe six basic preparation skills. For each, give an example where it's used.
2) Define the following medium preparation skills:
   a) creaming,   b) dehydrating,   c) kneading,   d) puréeing,   e) rubbing-in,   f) weighing.
3) Describe how you'd melt chocolate using a bain-marie. Give one benefit of this technique.
4) Apart from using a bain-marie, describe three other complex preparation skills.
5) Name seven techniques that can be used to chop ingredients.
   For each technique, state whether it is a medium or a complex skill.
6) Briefly describe three knife techniques that are used for meat and fish. State the level of each technique.

Cooking Techniques (p.76-77)

7) Draw three big boxes and label them 'basic', 'medium' and 'complex'. Now, try to think of as many cooking skills as you can, and put them in the correct box, depending on the level of the skill.
8) Define six cooking methods that use water.
9) Define six cooking methods that use dry heat.
10) What is frying? Describe three different frying techniques.
11) Describe two methods that can be used when making sauces.
12) Briefly describe the following techniques that can be used when making desserts:
    a) tempering,   b) caramelising.
13) Give three methods that can be used to preserve food.

Presentation Skills and Techniques (p.78-79)

14) Give three features of a serving dish you should consider when thinking about presentation.
15) Describe how you can use colour and layout to make a dish look more appealing.
16) Describe four different plating styles and draw a quick sketch showing each one.
17) Why is it important that portions aren't too big or too small?
18) Describe what accompaniments are and why they're used.
19) Give an example of each of the following types of accompaniment:
    a) savoury carbohydrate,   b) vegetable,   c) savoury sauce,   d) sweet sauce.
20) Describe the difference between garnishes and decorations.
21) Give four examples of sweet garnishes. Now do the same for savoury garnishes.

Food Safety Practices (p.80)

22) Give three personal hygiene and safety practices you should follow when you're in the kitchen.
23) Give four examples of good food hygiene practices.
24) What should you do if someone gets ill or injured whilst you're in the kitchen?
25) What should you do if there's a fire whilst you're in the kitchen?

Reviewing Dishes and Performance (p.81-82)

26) Briefly describe the following areas you should consider when reviewing a dish you have created:
    a) dish selection,   b) dish production,   c) presentation,   d) organoleptic qualities,
    e) health, safety and hygiene,   f) waste,   g) improvements.
27) Name four key skills you should think about when writing a review of your performance during the controlled assessment. Give one example of each.

About the Assessments

Hurray — you've made it to the end of the book. Here's one final page on what to expect in the written exam and the controlled assessment. Let's go...

Page 2 has details about what's covered in Unit 1 and Unit 2.

There are Different Question Types in the Exam

- In the exam, you could be tested on anything from Unit 1 — that's all the stuff covered on pages 3-53.
- Some questions will ask you to recall information to show you know and understand what you've learnt.
- In other questions, you'll be given some details about a scenario or an establishment, and you'll have to apply your knowledge and skills to the situation presented in the question.
- You'll also need to show that you can analyse (examine in detail) and evaluate (use evidence to make judgements and conclusions) information given to you.
- There are different question styles you could get in the exam, from completing tables to ones that need an extended written answer. Whatever the question, there are some important things you should remember:

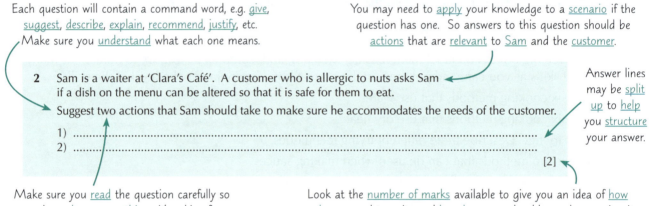

Each question will contain a command word, e.g. give, suggest, describe, explain, recommend, justify, etc. Make sure you understand what each one means.

You may need to apply your knowledge to a scenario if the question has one. So answers to this question should be actions that are relevant to Sam and the customer.

Answer lines may be split up to help you structure your answer.

Make sure you read the question carefully so you know how many things it's asking for.

Look at the number of marks available to give you an idea of how much you need to write and how long you should spend answering it.

The Controlled Assessment has Practical and Written Elements

The controlled assessment could test anything in Unit 2 (p.54-83). Knowledge of the content in Unit 1 is also needed for this assessment. You'll be given an assignment brief and then four tasks that you'll need to complete in the 12 hours:

- TASK 1 — You'll need to choose two dishes that are suitable for the two groups of customers given in the brief. You'll need to explain how the dishes meet the nutritional needs of these groups and how cooking methods will affect the nutritional value of the dishes (see pages 54-63).

- TASK 2 — You'll need to discuss the factors that led you to your choice of dishes (see pages 65-69). Then you'll create a production plan (p.70-72) for how you are going to produce the two dishes.

- TASK 3 — Once your plan is complete, you'll need to prepare, cook and present your dishes. You'll be assessed on your skills, as well as the health, safety and hygiene practices you follow (p.74-80).

- TASK 4 — Once you've served your dishes, you'll need to produce a written report evaluating the dishes you create and reviewing your overall performance in the controlled assessment. There are details of what your report should include on pages 81-82.

You'll be given a suggested time in which to complete each task. You can split the 12 hours between the tasks however you like, but it's probably best not to deviate too far from the recommended times — if you spend too long planning your menu, you might not leave enough time for cooking the dishes.

I always give 100% — that's why I lost my job as an exam marker...

For both assessments, make sure you read things really, really carefully. If you rush, you can easily miss important information or misunderstand something, and this might mean you lose valuable marks.

Index

3 Rs 20, 68

A

AA rosette awards 9
accident forms 32, 41
accidents 32, 39–41, 80
accompaniments 79
adverts 22, 36
allergens 47, 51
allergies 34, 45, 47, 62, 68
anaphylaxis 45, 47
apprentices (kitchen) 12
apprenticeships 14, 16
apps 21, 36
aspartame 46

B

back of house 12, 24–26
  dress code 29
bacteria 43–45, 47, 48, 50
balanced diets 58, 67
banquet service 7
basal metabolic rate (BMR) 60, 61
benefits (employment) 16
best before dates 48, 51, 71
biological contamination 43, 45
  bacterial 45, 47
bonuses (employment) 16
broadcast media 22
buffet service 8
business customers 35

C

cafeteria service 8
calcium 56, 59, 60
carbohydrates 55, 58, 59, 61
  complex 55
  simple 55
carbon footprints 19
cardiovascular disease (CVD) 62
caretakers 11
cashless payments 21
casual contracts 15
chambermaids 11
chefs de partie 12
chemical contamination 43, 45, 49
chilling (food) 50, 76, 77
cleaners 11
colours (presentation) 67, 78
commercial businesses 3, 5, 6, 17
commis chefs 12
commodity lists 70
competitions (media) 22
competitors 36, 37
concierges 10
Consumer Rights Act 33

contamination 43–49, 71
contingencies 72
contracts 15, 16
Control of Substances Hazardous to Health (COSHH) 32, 39
cooking techniques 76, 77
cooling (food) 44, 72
costs 17, 18, 65
counter service 8, 24
creativity 78
critical control points (CCPs) 43, 44
cross-contamination 48, 49, 71
customer
  demographics 37
  expectations 36
  needs 33–35, 37, 66
  reviews 22, 36
  rights 33

D

daily energy requirements 61
dairy products 47, 58, 62
danger zone 50
decision-making 82
decorations 79
defrosting 50
delivery notes 31
delivery records 32
dietary fibre 56, 60
dietary reference values (DRVs) 58
dietary requirements 34, 68
dish production 81
dish selection 81
disposable incomes 18, 34
dovetailing (sequencing) 70, 82
dress codes 29

E

economy 18, 34
energy
  from food 54, 55, 59–61
  saving (sustainability) 20, 68
Environmental Health Officer (EHO) 52
environmental impacts 19, 20, 68
Equality Act 33
equipment
  large-scale 27
  protective 28, 40
  quality of 29
  safety 28, 39, 71
  small-scale 28
  specialist 69, 70
evaluations 81, 82
exchange rates 18
executive chefs 12

F

family-style service 7
fast food 6, 8, 21
fats 54, 58–61
  saturated 54
  unsaturated 54
fibre 56, 60
fire safety 39, 80
first aid boxes 28, 80
First In, First Out (FIFO) 30, 48
food groups 58
food hazards 43–45
food hygiene 80
  ratings 9
food labelling 51
food laws 51, 52
food miles 19
food poisoning 45, 47
food safety 51, 52, 71
fossil fuels 19
freezing (food) 50, 76, 77
front of house 10, 24, 25
  dress code 29
  manager 10
full-time contracts 15

G

garnishes 79
gluten intolerance 46, 62
Good Food Guide 9
greenhouse gases 19
guéridon service 7

H

Hazard Analysis and Critical Control Points (HACCP) 43, 44
hazards 32, 39, 41–45
  symbols 39
head waiters 10
health and safety 26, 28, 29, 32, 39, 40, 52, 71, 80, 81
Health and Safety at Work Act (HASAWA) 39
Health and Safety Executive (HSE) 40, 42
high-risk foods 44, 47, 48, 50
holiday entitlement 15, 16
home delivery 8
hot holding (food) 44, 72
hotels 5, 9, 25, 35
housekeeping 11, 13
hygiene 43, 49, 51, 71, 80, 81
  ratings 9

Index

I

improvements (evaluating performance) 81, 82
ingredients 65, 70, 71
internet 22
intolerances 45, 46, 62, 68
invoices 31
iron (nutrient) 56, 59, 60
   deficiency 62

K

kitchen
   assistant 12
   brigade 12
   layout 26
   porters 12
   workflow 25, 26
knife techniques 75

L

lactose intolerance 46, 62
layout (presentation) 78
leisure customers 35
life-stages 59, 60
lifestyles (customer needs) 34
local residents 35

M

macro-nutrients 54, 61
magnesium 56
maintenance (housekeeping) 11
maîtres d'hôtel 10
management 10, 13
Manual Handling Operations Regulations 40
marketing 13
media 22, 36
medical conditions 62, 68
menu planning 65–69
Michelin stars 9
micro-nutrients 54
microorganisms 45, 50
minerals 56
mise en place 71
MSG 46

N

National Minimum Wage 16
non-commercial businesses 3, 4
non-residential businesses 3, 4, 6, 24
non-starch polysaccharide (NSP) 56
nutritional
   guidance 67
   information 34, 51
   life-stages 59, 60
   needs 34, 59, 60

O

ordering forms 31
organisation (evaluating performance) 82
organoleptic qualities 67, 81

P

part-time contracts 15
pastry chefs 12
pensions 16
personal attributes 10–13
personal protective equipment (PPE) 28, 40
Personal Protective Equipment at Work Regulations (PPER) 40
personal service 8
pescatarians 63
physical activity level (PAL) 61
physical contamination 45, 49
planning (evaluating performance) 82
planning production 70–72
plate service 7
plating styles 78
plongeurs 12
portion control 20, 65, 78
potassium 56
pregnancy 47, 58, 62
preparation techniques 74, 75
presentation 67, 72
   evaluating performance 81
   skills 78, 79
printed media 22
profits 17, 65
proteins 55, 58, 59, 61

Q

qualifications 14
quality points 70

R

ratings 9
receptionists 10
recycling 20, 68
reducing (sustainability) 20, 68
reheating 43, 44, 50
religious beliefs 63, 68
Reporting of Injuries, Diseases and Dangerous Occurrences Regulations (RIDDOR) 40
residential businesses 3–5, 25
restaurant standards 9
reusing (sustainability) 20, 68
reviews 81, 82
risk assessments 42–44
risks 42

S

safety 26, 28, 29, 32, 39, 40, 52, 71, 80, 81
salaries 16
seasonal contracts 15
seasonality 19, 68
services types 7, 8
serving dishes 78
sick pay 16
silver service 7
skills 69, 74–79
social media 22, 36
sodium 56
software 21
sous-chefs 12
star ratings 9
stock control 21, 30, 31
storage 25–27, 30, 50, 70
sustainability 19, 20, 68
symptoms 45–47

T

table service 7, 24
takeaways 8
technology 21, 30
temperature control 50, 72
temporary contracts 15
time management 70, 82
tips (benefit) 16
tray service 8
trolley service 8
type 2 diabetes 62

U

uniforms 29
use-by dates 48, 51, 71, 80
utensils 28

V

valets 10
Value Added Tax (VAT) 18
value for money 28, 36, 66
vegans 63, 68
vegetarians 63, 68
vitamins 54, 57, 59, 60

W

wages 16
waiting staff 10
waste 20, 26, 68, 81
water 56, 59, 61
work experience 14
workflow 24–26
Working Times Regulations 15

Z

zero-hours contracts 15